THE TRAIL OF CRICKET'S HOLY GRAIL

Devendra Prabhudesai has worked across sectors and handled a diverse range of responsibilities in a career spanning twenty years. He is an author, screenwriter and anchor. He was Manager, Media Relations & Corporate Affairs at the Board of Control for Cricket in India (BCCI) from January 2008 to July 2015. He designed and scripted India's first Heritage Cricket Walk for HopOnIndia in 2017. He is presently Head of Corporate Relations, and Research Associate at the International Institute of Sports Management (IISM). Devendra lives in Mumbai with his wife and children. This is his eighth book.

Among the author's previous works are *The Nice Guy Who Finished First, a biography of Rahul Dravid* (2005), *SMG, a biography of Sunil Manohar Gavaskar* (2009) and *Hero: A Biography of Sachin Ramesh Tendulkar* (2017).

THE WORLD CUP,
FROM 1975 TO 2019

Devendra Prabhudesai

RUPA

Published by
Rupa Publications India Pvt. Ltd 2019
7/16, Ansari Road, Daryaganj
New Delhi 110002

Sales centres:
Allahabad Bengaluru Chennai
Hyderabad Jaipur Kathmandu
Kolkata Mumbai

Copyright © Devendra Prabhudesai 2019

All rights reserved.

No part of this publication may be reproduced, transmitted,
or stored in a retrieval system, in any form or by any means,
electronic, mechanical, photocopying, recording or otherwise,
without the prior permission of the publisher.

ISBN: 978-93-5333-393-5

First impression 2019

10 9 8 7 6 5 4 3 2 1

The moral right of the author has been asserted.

Printed at HT Media Ltd, Gr. Noida

This book is sold subject to the condition that it shall not,
by way of trade or otherwise, be lent, resold, hired out, or otherwise circulated,
without the publisher's prior consent, in any form of binding or cover other than
that in which it is published.

To
AAI, ANU & IRA,
the three women in my life

CONTENTS

Introduction: Taking Guard	ix
1. 1975: A Flying Start	1
2. 1979: Knights of the Caribbean	10
3. 1983: The Upset of the Millennium	19
4. 1987: The Start of the Global Journey	29
5. 1992: Cornered Tigers	41
6. 1996: The Pride of Lankan Lions	51
7. 1999: A Tale of Seven 'Finals'	61
8. 2003: Awesome Aussies—I	73
9. 2007: Awesome Aussies—II	85
10. 2011: Dhoni's Devils	94
11. 2015: Advance Australia!	105
12. India v Pakistan: Six out of Six!	115
13 2019—Back to Blighty	126
Bibliography	137

INTRODUCTION: TAKING GUARD

The history of cricket, replete as it is with startling occurrences and unforeseen twists, took a significant turn in July 1973. A couple of days before the conclusion of the inaugural Women's Cricket World Cup that was hosted and won by England, the International Cricket Conference (ICC)[1] which at that point was the apex global organization for men's cricket only, accepted the proposal of England's Test and County Cricket Board (TCCB)[2] to organize a (men's) World Cup in 1975.

A little over two decades before this development, the inter-club Padmakar Talim Shield Tournament was instituted in Mumbai, India, in 1951. The first-ever One Day 'limited overs'

---

[1] The ICC was renamed the International Cricket Council in 1989.

[2] The TCCB and the National Cricket Association (NCA) were amalgamated into the England and Wales Cricket Board (ECB) in 1997.

cricket tournament in the world, the Talim Shield, made an impression without threatening to overshadow the traditional, 'multi-day' version of the sport, in India's cricketing capital. The circumstances were decidedly different in England in the early 1960s, when the authorities conceived of a One Day limited overs tournament to entice the spectators, who had turned their backs on the traditional format, back to cricket. The inter-county Gillette Cup, the first edition of which was played in 1963, was a runaway success and it ended up achieving its desired objective, which was to improve turnouts for first class matches.

The popularity of the Gillette Cup and England's triumph in the FIFA World Cup in 1966 prompted some cricket administrators and fans to try and put together a 'Cricket World Cup' in the limited overs format. However, nothing concrete materialized until a seminal incident in January 1971. The first three days of the third Test of the 1970-71 Ashes at the Melbourne Cricket Ground were washed out and the match was officially abandoned. The skies cleared on the scheduled fifth day of the Test and the 2 teams were persuaded to play a 'One Day' 40(8-ball)-overs-a-side match to whet the appetite of the cricket-starved Melbournians. Australia won what came to be regarded as the first official One Day International (ODI) by 5 wickets and the spectators lapped up the action. This prompted the authorities to schedule as many as 3 ODIs during the next Ashes series, which was played in England in 1972. The first-

INTRODUCTION: TAKING GUARD

ever ODI series turned out to be a hit. The TCCB then set up a committee to work on a plan for a World Cup, the efforts of which were acknowledged and praised by the ICC a year later. The stage was thus set for a competition of 60-overs-a-side matches that would feature all the Test-playing nations of the time, plus 2 associate members of the ICC.

To say that cricket's ultimate quadrennial event for men has come a long way since its first edition in 1975 would be an understatement. The first edition, hosted by England, spanned two weeks, featured 8 teams and comprised 15 matches. The eleventh edition, co-hosted by Australia and New Zealand in 2015, spanned forty-four days, featured 14 teams and comprised 49 matches.

The tournament has undergone many a makeover—in terms of the format, complexion and even the name—as has the game of cricket itself, in the forty-four years from 1975 to 2019.

When the inaugural World Cup got underway in 1975, the game seemed to be in the pink of health, but there was discontent beneath the surface. Players from all over the world were bringing in the crowds and augmenting the coffers of their respective boards, but they were upset at being underpaid and treated patronizingly by the establishment. However, this did not come in the way of their producing some magnificent cricket in the first edition of the World Cup. The success of the tournament underscored One Day cricket's newfound status as the game's biggest box office attraction.

Nearly two years after the first World Cup, the sport was rocked by its biggest controversy since the Bodyline controversy of 1932-33. Kerry Packer, an Australian media magnate, created a parallel body called World Series Cricket and signed up over 50 top cricketers from across the world to join his enterprise. The establishment was rattled and forced to extend an olive branch to the players. World Series Cricket ensured that the players started earning what they deserved; it also made them, and in the process, the sport itself, more professional.

The West Indies, who won the World Cup in 1975, proved in the second edition of the tournament in 1979 that they were as capable of staying at the summit as they were of scaling it. All those who believed that the team could not get any better than what they were at the end of the 1970s were forced to do a rethink when they went fifteen years without losing a Test series, from 1980 to 1995. The one prominent blip during this period was their loss to India in the final of the third World Cup.

India's conquest of the 1983 edition set in process a series of events that culminated in the new millennium. The country that loves cricket like no other replaced England, cricket's birthplace, as the hub of the sport.

As unexpected as India's victory in 1983 were the triumphs

INTRODUCTION: TAKING GUARD

by Australia and Pakistan in 1987 and 1992 respectively. The consistency of the Sri Lankans in every aspect of the game enabled them to win the tournament in 1996.

The seventh edition of the tournament and the first to be played in England since 1983 heralded the start of a new era in 1999. Australia's extraordinary campaign flagged off a ten-year phase during which the men from Down Under dominated the sport like very few teams before them had. They made a mockery of the 'law of averages' in the 2003 and 2007 editions of the World Cup. Their victorious run was finally halted by India in the tenth World Cup in 2011. However, the Aussies bounced back in the next edition of the competition. Michael Clarke's side emulated Mahendra Singh Dhoni's team of 2011 by winning the World Cup on home turf in 2015.

After having travelled the length and breadth of the cricketing world, the World Cup will return to England, where it all began, in May 2019. The twelfth edition of the quadrennial competition will span forty-seven days and comprise 10 teams and 48 matches.

Just like it was in 1975, the game seems to be in excellent shape on the face of it in 2019, but the reality is that a problem is simmering. The advent of the Twenty20 format has changed outlooks, on as well as off the field. Not very long ago, the 50-over format was being credited for transforming defensive mindsets into assertive ones, the effect of which had spilt over into Test cricket, the apogee of the sport. It was noted that teams were playing 'to win' even in the traditional version and they were not averse to taking calculated risks to achieve that objective. Today, the same brand of 'Fifty50' cricket has been branded a 'misfit' in an age of instant gratification. It is being claimed by some that spectators and TV viewers no longer have the time, inclination and patience to sit through the phase between the 16th and 40th overs of a 50-over innings, wherein the batting side aims to build on its start by maintaining a steady but unexciting scoring rate and keeps wickets in hand for the assault in the slog overs. Twenty20, its supporters argue, has taken precisely this 'uneventful' phase of a 50-over innings out of the equation. It is being contended by detractors of 50-over cricket matches that the traditional version—Test cricket—has a niche audience, and at the other end of the spectrum are those who are crazy about Twenty20, the newest and shortest limited overs format. Fifty50 apparently has no place in the scheme of things anymore.

The proliferation of Twenty20 leagues across the world and recent developments in the islands whose team won the first 2 World Cups have triggered a debate that will only get bigger in the months and years to come: will cricket go the soccer way with more and more players according more importance to their clubs than their countries? As Twenty20 gets bigger, it is more than likely that players from other regions will follow

INTRODUCTION: TAKING GUARD

the footsteps of the cricketers from the Caribbean, by becoming 'freelancers'.

Be that as it may, the ICC Cricket World Cup 2019 will not give the players and fans the time and space to ponder over these issues. Cricket's twelfth World Cup promises to be a spectacular celebration of the sport and all the values it represents. Will the tournament make as emphatic a statement on behalf of the 'shorter' version of the game as was made by the inaugural edition in 1975, and thereby silence critics of the format? Will the twelfth World Cup emulate the 1983 edition, which was also played in England, by signalling a shift in cricket's 'world order'? Or will the 2019 World Cup usher in a new era dominated by a single team, like the 1999 tournament that was also hosted by England?

We will find out soon!

1

1975: A FLYING START

THE INAUGURAL EDITION of the World Cup was blessed by the gods, with the clouds that usually hover over English grounds taking a break and letting the latter bask in sunshine. All the six Test-playing teams of the time—Australia, England, India, New Zealand, Pakistan and the West Indies—participated, as did Sri Lanka, then an associate member of the ICC. The eighth side was East Africa—a combined team of cricketers from Kenya, Tanzania, Uganda and Zambia.

The limited overs version was treated as nothing more than an abbreviated form of the traditional variety in the first World Cup. 30-yard circles and field restrictions had not been thought of at the time. The teams also did not tinker with their batting and bowling orders or look to play limited overs 'specialists' at the expense of those who were natural choices for Test cricket. The only tangible differences between the longer and shorter formats were the duration of a match and a restriction on the number of overs to be bowled by a single bowler—12. Two hours into the innings of the team batting first, the teams broke for lunch. There was a ten-minute interval for the changeover at the end of an innings, and play was halted for tea, two hours into the innings of the team batting second.

England were touted as the favourites for the simple reason that their players had a lot more experience of limited overs cricket than those from other countries in which limited overs cricket was yet to make an impact. The English started well but fell short of a place in the final. The West Indies batted, bowled and fielded superbly, and most importantly, held their nerve in tense situations, to take the title.

FACTFILE: PRUDENTIAL WORLD CUP 1975

Host: England

Duration: 7–21 June

Participating teams: 8

Matches: 15

Venues: 6

Title sponsor: Prudential Assurance Company (£100,000)

1975: A FLYING START

Trophy: A sterling silver trophy that weighed 2.5 kg and was 47 cm high

Format: Each match was a 60-overs-a-side affair. The eight teams were divided into two groups of four each. Each side played the other three in its group once and the top two sides from both groups qualified for the semi-finals.

Mascot: Jiminy Cricket (a Walt Disney character)

Total prize money: £9,000

Prize money for the winners: £4,000

Groups –

A: **England**[1], **New Zealand**, India, East Africa

B: **West Indies**, **Australia**, Pakistan, Sri Lanka

Winners: West Indies

Runners-up: Australia

Losing semi-finalists: England (beaten by Australia) and New Zealand (beaten by the West Indies)

Highest scorer: Glenn Turner (New Zealand)—333 runs@166.50 from four matches, inclusive of 2 centuries

Turner's highest score: 171 (not out) v East Africa at Birmingham

---

[1]The teams marked in bold qualified for the semi-finals.

Highest wicket-taker: Gary Gilmour (Australia)—11 wickets @5.63 from two matches, inclusive of one 6-wicket haul and one 5-wicket haul

Gilmour's best bowling figures: 6/14 v England at Leeds in the semi-final

CLASSIC CLASHES

Group B: West Indies v Pakistan, Edgbaston, Birmingham, 11 June 1975

This was a knockout encounter for Pakistan, who had lost to Australia in their first match of the competition. Majid Khan, Pakistan's stand-in skipper in the absence of the injured Asif Iqbal, won the toss and elected to bat. The Asians gave a good account of themselves, scoring 266/7 in their innings. Their bowlers then kept pegging away at the West Indian batsmen, not allowing partnerships to build, and sending them back to the pavilion at regular intervals. Deryck Murray, the wicketkeeper-batsman, kept his cool, even as the wickets kept falling at the other end. He and Vanburn Holder added 37 for the 9th wicket before the latter fell in the 46th over. At that stage, the target was 64 runs away and Pakistan needed only 1 more wicket to win. Murray inspired Andy Roberts, the No. 11 batsman, to put a price on his wicket. The pair nudged the ball around and ran splendidly,

1975: A FLYING START

even as the Pakistanis panicked. Majid Khan gambled by going for the kill and getting Sarfraz Nawaz, his most successful bowler, to complete his quota of 12 overs. However, West Indies' last pair was undeterred and made the most of Sarfraz's early exit from the attack. Much to the delight of their teammates and supporters, who found their voice after being despondent for the better part of the day, Murray and Roberts took their team home in the penultimate over.

Result: Pakistan [266/7 (60)] lost to West Indies [267/9 (59.4)] by 1 wicket.

First semi-final: Australia v England, Headingley, Leeds, 18 June 1975

Ian Chappell, the Australian captain, won the toss and put the opposition in to bat on a juicy wicket. The spectators were then treated to one of the greatest exhibitions of seam and swing bowling. Gary Gilmour, Australia's left-handed paceman, exploited the conditions brilliantly to take 6 wickets in next to no time. He trapped Dennis Amiss, Keith Fletcher, Frank Hayes and Alan Knott leg before, bowled Barry Wood and had Tony Greig spectacularly caught by Rodney Marsh. England, 36/6 at one stage, huffed and puffed their way to 93, thanks to their captain Mike Denness (27) and Geoff Arnold (18*). With

---

*not out

only 94 to win, it seemed that the Australians had all the time in the world to seal their spot in the first-ever World Cup final. However, all those who expected an early finish were in for a shock. What was good enough for Gilmour was certainly good enough for England's pacers John Snow, Geoff Arnold and Chris Old, all of whom knew exactly how to operate at Headingley. Arnold took 1, Snow 2 and Old 3 wickets to reduce Australia to 39/6. The fall of the 6th wicket brought the man who had been England's nemesis earlier in the day to the crease. It was Gary Gilmour's day and he wasn't going to let anybody spoil it. He and Doug Walters worked their way towards the target. The Australians got there without any further loss, with Gilmour scoring an undefeated 28 to add to his 6/14 with the ball.

Result: England [93 (36.2)] lost to Australia [94/6 (28.4)] by 4 wickets.

Final: West Indies v Australia, Lord's, London, 21 June 1975

The summit clash of the first World Cup featured all the elements that characterize a humdinger—outstanding cricket, drama and errors of judgement at key stages. Ian Chappell won the toss and elected to field on a bouncy strip. The boisterous West Indian supporters were silenced when Roy Fredericks, the West Indies opener, hooked Dennis Lillee out of the ground, but trod on his wicket in the process and had to go. Clive Lloyd arrived at the crease at 50/3 and proceeded to

1975: A FLYING START

score a belligerent 102. Their captain's pyrotechnics enabled the West Indies to finish at 291/8. The Australians seemed on course when an Antiguan answering to the name of Vivian Richards displayed his verve in the field and ran as many as three batsmen out, including the Chappell brothers, Australia's bulwarks. The lower order struggled, and when Jeff Thomson, the No. 11, joined Lillee in the 53rd over, the Australians still needed 59. The pair did not panic, and kept the scoreboard ticking. There was chaos when Thomson was caught off a no-ball and the spectators invaded the field, thinking that it was all over; Fredericks, who had taken the 'catch', then tried to hit the stumps to affect a run out, but missed, and the batsmen ran and ran. It took a while for order to be restored and the Australians were awarded 3 runs. The equation was down to 18 runs from 9 balls when Thomson became the fifth Australian to be run out that evening.

Result: West Indies [291-8 (60)] beat Australia [274 (58.4)] by 17 runs.

THE 1975 WORLD CUP QUIZ

1. Although as many as four matches were played on 7 June 1975, the first day of the competition, the Group A match between England and India got top billing as it was played at Lord's, the headquarters of the sport. Who is credited

with scoring the first century in a World Cup match?
2. Who was the first of five Australians to be run out in the final?
3. Who finished with bowling figures of 12-8-6-1 in a league match of the competition?
4. I represented East Africa in the 1975 World Cup. My son represented another team in two World Cups. Who am I?
5. I scored a half century in the final, which was also my last international match. Who am I?
6. The Sri Lankans gave Australia a brief scare in their league match before Jeff Thomson, one of the most feared pacemen of all time, forced two of their batsmen to retire hurt. Sunil Wettimuny, who was hit on his right instep, was one of them. Name the other.
7. Two Pakistan players made their ODI debuts in the league match against the West Indies at Birmingham. Parvez Mir was one of them. Name the other.
8. I won the individual award despite being on the losing side in a league match of the tournament. Who am I?
9. Who was West Indies' most successful bowler in the semi-final against New Zealand?
10. 4, 4, 4, 4, 4, 1, 4, 6, 0, 4—which batsman's scoring sequence was this, off 10 consecutive deliveries bowled by Dennis Lillee in a league match?

1975: A FLYING START

THE 1975 WORLD CUP QUIZ: ANSWERS

1. Dennis Amiss (England). He scored 137 against India.
2. Alan Turner
3. Bishan Singh Bedi's (India) bowling analysis against East Africa read 12-8-6-1.
4. Don Pringle. His son Derek represented England in the 1987 and 1992 World Cups.
5. Rohan Kanhai (West Indies). He scored 55 in the final.
6. Duleep Mendis. He had scored an enterprising 32 when he could not get out of the way of a Jeff Thomson delivery that rose awkwardly from a good length and hit him on the forehead.
7. Javed Miandad
8. Sarfraz Nawaz of Pakistan won the individual award for his 4/44 against West Indies at Birmingham. His team lost the match by 1 wicket, despite his heroics.
9. Bernard Julien, the left-arm paceman. He took 4/27 and hastened New Zealand's demise for 158. The West Indies won the match by 5 wickets.
10. Alvin Kallicharran of the West Indies put Lillee to the sword in an innings of 78 against Australia at the Oval, London.

2

1979: KNIGHTS OF THE CARIBBEAN

BUOYED BY THE success of the first World Cup, the ICC scheduled another four years later. The rapprochement between the establishment and Kerry Packer was worked out weeks before the second World Cup got underway in England in 1979. Despite the disbanding of World Series Cricket, Australia chose not to pick their 'Packer' players for the 1979 World Cup. Pakistan and the West Indies were far more pragmatic.

The second edition was played along the same lines as its predecessor in 1975. The format was unchanged, as were the tactics. Seven of the eight teams were the same as in 1975, the exception being Canada, who qualified along with Sri Lanka by making it to the final of the 1979 ICC Trophy. The Sri Lankans went on to create history, becoming the first associate member to beat a full member in an ODI, when they outplayed India by 47 runs in a Group B match.

The inexperienced Australians crashed out at the group stage, while Pakistan qualified for the semi-finals for the first time. The New Zealanders stumbled at that stage for the second time in succession, this time against the hosts. England fancied their chances of winning the title, but their opponents in the summit clash were unstoppable. The West Indies, defending champions and an extraordinary outfit, retained the title by outdoing their own performance of 1975. The success of the second edition inspired the ICC to formally decide that the World Cup would be a quadrennial affair.

FACTFILE: PRUDENTIAL WORLD CUP 1979

Host: England

Duration: 9–23 June

Participating teams: 8

Matches: 15

Venues: 6

Title sponsor: Prudential Assurance Company (£250,000)

THE TRAIL OF CRICKET'S HOLY GRAIL

Trophy: Same as in 1975

Format: Same as in 1975

Prize money: £25,900 (just over 10% of the sponsorship amount)

Prize money for the winners: £10,000

Groups–

A: England, Pakistan, Australia, Canada

B: West Indies, New Zealand, Sri Lanka, India

Winners: West Indies

Runners-up: England

Losing semi-finalists: Pakistan (beaten by the West Indies) and New Zealand (beaten by England)

Highest scorer: Gordon Greenidge (West Indies)—253 runs @84.33 from four matches, inclusive of a century and 2 fifties

Greenidge's highest score: 106* v India at Edgbaston, Birmingham

Highest wicket-taker: Mike Hendrick (England)—10 wickets @14.9

Hendrick's best bowling figures: 4/15 v Pakistan at Headingley, Leeds

1979: KNIGHTS OF THE CARIBBEAN

CLASSIC CLASHES

Group A: England v Pakistan, Headingley, Leeds, 16 June 1979

Both teams were assured of a semi-final berth, but they still wanted to beat each other in their last Group A match for obvious reasons. The winner of the encounter would get to play New Zealand, the second-ranked team from Group B, in the semis, while the loser would have to square off against the mighty West Indies, who had topped that group. Asif Iqbal, the captain of Pakistan, won the toss and elected to bowl. Imran Khan, Pakistan's pace spearhead, took 2 quick wickets and his colleagues maintained the pressure. England were a sorry 118/8 when the two Bobs—Taylor and Willis—came together for a match-defining stand. They enabled their side to finish 165/9. In response, the Pakistani openers put on a quick 27 before the top and middle order caved in. Mike Hendrick took 4 wickets and Ian Botham bagged 2 to leave the batting side tottering at 34/6. Asif Iqbal was aided first by Wasim Raja and then by Imran Khan in his bid to resurrect the innings. Imran took over the mantle once the captain fell at 115; only 51 runs were needed and there were plenty of overs left. As the Pakistanis inched closer, Mike Brearley, the England captain, turned to Geoffrey Boycott's 'gentle' medium pacers, having realized that he would need to keep overs from his main bowlers in reserve, in case things got too tight. Boycott delivered by dismissing Wasim Bari and Sikander Bakht, Pakistan's No. 10 and No. 11 respectively.

Result: England [165/9 (60)] beat Pakistan [151 (56)] by 14 runs.

Second semi-final: West Indies v Pakistan, The Oval, London, 20 June 1979

Asif Iqbal would have regretted his decision to bowl after winning the toss when Gordon Greenidge and Desmond Haynes, the West Indies openers, put on 132. The holders amassed 293/6 in their allotted overs. Impressive as the total was, it wasn't beyond the reach of the Pakistanis, provided they batted to their potential. The left-handed Sadiq Mohammed was dismissed early, but Majid Khan, his opening partner, was in imperial form, as was Zaheer Abbas. The two batsmen, both epitomes of elegance, made batting look ridiculously easy against one of the most formidable bowling attacks of all time. With 20 overs to go, the batting team having 9 wickets in hand and the required rate a comfortable 5 per over, Clive Lloyd figured that he needed to do something different. He asked Vivian Richards to bowl his off-breaks and persisted with him despite his going for runs. He also instructed Colin Croft, one of the four pacemen at his disposal, to bowl a leg stump line. So well did Croft do what was expected of him that he frustrated Zaheer into nicking him down the leg side to the wicketkeeper. Haroon Rashid, the next man in, struggled to get going, and that only intensified the pressure on Majid, who was eventually caught in the covers, also off Croft. From 176/1, Pakistan declined to 187/4. With new batsmen in the middle, the West Indies bowlers found their mojo back and shut their opponents out of the match.

Result: West Indies [293/6 (60)] beat Pakistan [250 (56.2)] by 43 runs.

Final: West Indies v England, Lord's, London, 23 June 1979

England started well. Brearley won the toss and let his bowlers make first use of the bowler friendly conditions, and then Derek Randall's alacrity in the field accounted for Gordon Greenidge, the tournament's top scorer. The Windies were a shaky 99/4 when Collis King joined Vivian Richards. This was the turning point of the match, as the duo tore the English attack apart with a stand of 139 in 77 minutes. King departed in the 51st over for 86, scored off only 66 balls. 'King' Richards carried on and completed his hundred. He batted into the final over and was on strike when Mike Hendrick ran in to bowl the last ball of the innings. Anticipating a yorker, Richards opened himself up well before the bowler delivered the ball and took it on the full, depositing it over the square leg fence. The West Indies finished 286/9, of which Richards' contribution was 138. Brearley and Boycott, the England openers, put on 129, but they took too much time to score those runs and left their colleagues with too much to do against the West Indies bowling. Graham Gooch did his best in a knock of 32 off 28 balls, but once he was bowled by Joel Garner, a giant of a paceman from the island of Barbados, the writing was on the wall for England. Garner took 5 wickets from 11 balls to ensure the speedy termination of England's innings.

Result: West Indies [286/9 (60)] beat England [194 (51)] by 92 runs.

THE 1979 WORLD CUP QUIZ

1. My 92 runs and 5 wickets ensured that I was one of the most successful all-rounders in the tournament. Who am I?
2. Who kept wicket for India in the tournament?
3. My father represented India in Tests. I played for another country with distinction and appeared in the first two World Cups. Who am I?
4. Which venue had the dubious distinction of 'hosting' the first-ever World Cup match that was washed out without a ball being bowled?

1979: KNIGHTS OF THE CARIBBEAN

5. I made my international debut in the tournament and played a total of six ODIs till January 1980 before being ignored by the selectors for nearly a decade. I played my next ODI in October 1989. Who am I?
6. Two teams did not win a single match in the tournament. Canada was one. Name the other.
7. I was a specialist bowler and captained my country in the first two World Cups. I did not take a single wicket in the six matches that I played in the 1975 and 1979 World Cups. Who am I?
8. Three members of the West Indies XI that played the final went on a 'Rebel' tour of South Africa in 1982-83. Collis King and Alvin Kallicharran were two of them. Name the third.
9. I represented my country at cricket and rugby. I played in the 1979 World Cup and was inadvertently part of a controversy in February 1981. Who am I?
10. Name the cricketer who opened the bowling in the 1979 World Cup final and the batting in another World Cup final.

THE 1979 WORLD CUP QUIZ: ANSWERS

1. Geoffrey Boycott
2. Surender Khanna

3. Majid Khan (Pakistan). His father Jahangir Khan played four Tests for India in the 1930s.
4. The Oval, London (the league match between the West Indies and Sri Lanka)
5. Wayne Larkins (England)
6. India (lost to the West Indies, New Zealand and Sri Lanka by 9 wickets, 8 wickets and 47 runs respectively).
7. S. Venkataraghavan (India)
8. Colin Croft
9. Brian McKechnie of New Zealand took 9 wickets in the 1979 World Cup. He was on strike when Australia's Trevor Chappell bowled the infamous 'underarm' delivery at Melbourne in February 1981.
10. Ian Botham took the new ball in the 1979 World Cup final. He opened the batting with Graham Gooch in the 1992 World Cup final.

3

1983: THE UPSET OF THE MILLENNIUM

THE NUMBER OF venues was increased and league matches doubled for the third edition of the tournament in 1983, with each team playing the other three in its group twice instead of once. This was ostensibly done to minimize the possibility of a leading team's campaign being jeopardized because of 'one bad day at the office' and give it more matches in which to bounce back. The keenness of the authorities to build on the success of the first two editions was also a factor that prompted the tweaking of the format, of course. More matches obviously meant greater financial gains. Those behind the revised format would have felt vindicated when the tournament got underway with not one, but two upsets on the opening day itself. Australia were stunned by debutants Zimbabwe and the West Indies suffered their first defeat in a World Cup match after ten consecutive wins. Ironically, but quite appropriately for a tournament that had begun with two shock results, the third World Cup ended with one of the greatest upsets in sporting history. Kapil Dev's Indian team, which had beaten Clive Lloyd's 'Invincibles' on the opening day of the competition, stunned the two-time champions on its last day and returned home to a rapturous welcome. The other side whose World Cup dream was shattered by India was England, who had hosted the tournament for the third time in succession. The English dominated their group before going down to the eventual champions in the semi-final.

FACTFILE: PRUDENTIAL WORLD CUP 1983

Hosts: England and Wales

Duration: 9–25 June

Participating teams: 8

Matches: 27

Venues: 14 in England and 1 in Wales

Title sponsor: Prudential Assurance Company (£500,000)

1983: THE UPSET OF THE MILLENNIUM

Trophy: The same as in 1975 and 1979

Format: A team played the other three in its group twice and the top two sides from each group qualified for the semi-finals. With Sri Lanka winning 'full membership' of the ICC in 1981, the edition comprised seven Test-playing teams and one associate member in Zimbabwe.

Prize money: £66,200

Prize money for the winners: £20,000

Groups–

A: England, Pakistan, New Zealand, Sri Lanka

B: West Indies, India, Australia, Zimbabwe

Winners: India

Runners-up: West Indies

Losing semi-finalists: Pakistan (beaten by the West Indies) and England (beaten by India)

Highest scorer: David Gower (England)—384 runs @76.8 from seven matches, inclusive of a century and a half century.

Gower's highest score: 130 v Sri Lanka at County Ground, Taunton

Highest wicket-taker: Roger Binny (India)—18 wickets @18.6

Binny's best bowling figures: 4/29 v Australia at County Ground, Chelmsford

CLASSIC CLASHES

Group B: Zimbabwe v Australia, Trent Bridge, Nottingham, 9 June 1983

The debutants, who had qualified for the 1983 World Cup after winning the ICC Trophy for the associate members the previous year, were put in to bat by Kim Hughes, the captain of Australia. The Zimbabwe openers put on 55 before both fell at the same score. Duncan Fletcher, the captain, arrived at the wicket at 86/4, after 2 wickets had once again fallen at the same score. A fifth fell soon after, but all-rounders Kevin Curran and Ian Butchart rose to the occasion and rallied around their captain, who anchored the innings with a knock of 69. The Zimbabweans were aided by pedestrian fielding, with the Australians making a mess of several chances. Needing 240 to win, Australia were 77/2 at tea interval. The batsmen discovered after the resumption that runs were not easy to come by; the bowlers were giving nothing away and the fielders were backing them up brilliantly. Zimbabwe's adherence to the basics yielded rewards. The wickets started falling, with one Australian batsman after another succumbing to the pressure. The lower order did what it could, but it wasn't enough. 23 were required off the final over. Rodney Marsh, Australia's wicketkeeper-batsman, hit the first ball for a six, but he and Rodney Hogg could manage only 4 more runs off the remaining deliveries. Fletcher was the unanimous choice for the individual award for his 69 runs and 4 wickets.

Result: Zimbabwe [239/6 (60)] beat Australia [226/7 (60)] by 13 runs.

Group B: India v West Indies, Old Trafford, Manchester, 9 June 1983

The defending champions commenced their mission to complete a treble of triumphs with a match against a team that had won only one of its six World Cup matches till that point. The match started late due to rain and the West Indies had no hesitation in opting to bowl in overcast conditions after winning the toss. Yashpal Sharma, one of India's earliest limited overs stars, handled the fast bowlers with aplomb in an innings of 89. His teammates batted around him, and India had reason to be satisfied with their score of 262/8. The match spilt over into a second day, due to the delayed start on the first. The West Indies, who were 67/2 overnight with their openers back in the pavilion, lost Vivian Richards immediately after the resumption. That wicket had an inspirational effect on the Indians. The batsmen were undone by the swing and movement that the Indian bowlers extracted from the conditions, and when the 8th wicket fell at 130, the underdogs scented victory. However,

Andy Roberts launched a counter-attack, with support first from Michael Holding and then Joel Garner. The equation was down to a gettable 35 from 36 balls when Ravi Shastri, recalled to the attack after his colleagues had gone for runs, drew Garner out of his crease. The batsman swung and missed, and Syed Kirmani, the wicketkeeper, collected the ball and dislodged the bails. West Indies' unbeaten run had ended for good.

Result: India [262/8 (60)] beat the West Indies [228 (54.1)] by 34 runs.

Group B: India v Zimbabwe, Neville Ground, Tunbridge Wells, 18 June 1983

Australia and the West Indies regained lost ground after their defeats in their first matches of the competition. By the time the two 'giant-killers' of the opening day faced off for the second time in the competition, the Windies had already qualified for the semi-finals and Australia and India were level on points. The Indians were so sold on the idea of batting first and scoring heavily against Zimbabwe to keep their run rate ahead of Australia's that they elected to bat on a track that had a lot in it for bowlers, after winning the toss. The move backfired; the scoreboard read a sensational 9/4 when Kapil Dev, the captain, made his way to the wicket; it soon got to 17/5. The lower order hung on and the captain completed the most conservative

1983: THE UPSET OF THE MILLENNIUM

fifty of his career in the 36th over of the innings. The score had moved to 140/8 when all hell broke loose. Kapil Dev's decision to change gears ensured that the ball started disappearing to the corners of the ground and occasionally beyond it. His furious and ferocious onslaught took India to 266/8. He came in undefeated on 175, the highest individual score in the World Cup, ahead of Glenn Turner's 171 against East Africa in 1975. Kevin Curran, the all-rounder, did his best to keep Zimbabwe in the game, but he did not get the support he deserved, and the final wicket fell at 235.

Result: India [266/8 (50)] beat Zimbabwe [235 (57)] by 31 runs.

Final: India v West Indies, Lord's, London, 25 June 1983

An early finish seemed imminent when the Indians, who had been asked to bat, lost their sixth wicket with only 111 on the board. K. Srikkanth and Mohinder Amarnath batted well in tandem after Gavaskar's early dismissal, but the men from the Caribbean regained control once the second-wicket stand was broken. India's last 4 wickets added 72, thus ensuring that the defending champions had a little more than 3 runs an over to chase. Gordon Greenidge's exit, courtesy a banana inswinger by B.S. Sandhu brought in Vivian Richards, who appeared to be in a hurry to take his team home. He bashed and blasted his way to 33 before mistiming a pull off Madan Lal. Kapil Dev, running backwards from mid-wicket, judged the cherry's descent adroitly and completed an outstanding catch. Haynes had already fallen by then, and 9 runs after Richards' dismissal, the Indians struck twice, dismissing Larry Gomes and then Clive Lloyd. The unbelievable was unfolding. Faoud Bacchus was the sixth to go a little later, but Jeffrey Dujon and Malcolm Marshall batted sensibly to add 43 until Amarnath, one of the several all-rounders in the Indian line-up, dismissed both in quick succession. Roberts fell to Kapil Dev and the score was 140/9 when Amarnath won an appeal for leg before against Holding. Kapil's Devils had shocked not only the West Indies, but the entire cricketing world, their compatriots included.

Result: India [183 (54.4)] beat the West Indies [140 (52)] by 43 runs.

THE 1983 WORLD CUP QUIZ

1. Two Indian players took 2 catches each in the final. Kapil Dev was one of them. Name the other.
2. Who won the individual award for his 'captaincy' in a league match?
3. Name the umpire who completed a 'hat-trick' of appearances in a World Cup final.

1983: THE UPSET OF THE MILLENNIUM

4. How many wickets did Imran Khan, who led Pakistan, take in the tournament?
5. What dubious distinction did New Zealand's Martin Snedden achieve against England at the Oval?
6. Kim Hughes, Australia's captain, missed the match against India at Chelmsford, Essex, due to injury. Who led Australia in his absence?
7. Name the only playing member of the Indian squad who did not get to figure in a single match in the tournament.
8. Who scored his only ODI century in a league match against India at Nottingham?
9. I was part of a team that qualified for the semi-finals of a World Cup for the very first time in 1983. Twenty years later, I was coach of a team that made it to the semis of a World Cup for the first time. Who am I?
10. Who became the first bowler to take 7 wickets in an ODI during the tournament?

THE 1983 WORLD CUP QUIZ: ANSWERS

1. Sunil Gavaskar. He caught Larry Gomes and Malcolm Marshall off Madan Lal and Mohinder Amarnath respectively.
2. Bob Willis, the captain of England, was declared the winner of the individual award for his captaincy in

his team's second league match against Sri Lanka at Headingley, Leeds.

3. Harold 'Dickie' Bird, one of the most popular umpires of all time, stood in the first three World Cup finals. He officiated with Tom Spencer in 1975 and with Barrie Meyer in 1979 and 1983. He was also a part of the international umpiring panel for the 1987 World Cup and officiated in the semi-final between Pakistan and Australia at Lahore, among other matches.
4. None. A stress fracture of the shin forced him to play the tournament as a batsman.
5. He became the first bowler to concede 100-plus runs in an ODI. His final figures read 12–1–105–2.
6. David Hookes
7. Sunil Valson
8. Trevor Chappell
9. Sandeep Patil was part of the Indian team in 1983. He coached the Kenyan team in the 2003 edition.
10. Winston Davis (West Indies) took a match-winning 7/51 against Australia at Headingley, Leeds.

4

1987: THE START OF THE GLOBAL JOURNEY

THE BOARD OF Control for Cricket in India(BCCI) teamed up with its Pakistani counterpart to first question England's right to host the quadrennial edition 'by default' and then make a joint bid to host the fourth edition of the tournament in 1987. Predictably, there were those who scoffed at the idea of two countries that had gone to war thrice in less than four decades, working together. However, the Asian combination had the last laugh. On 19 July 1984, the ICC announced that the fourth World Cup would be played in India and Pakistan. The global journey of cricket's premier competition had well and truly begun.

The shorter days on the subcontinent warranted a reduction in the number of overs. The first World Cup to be played outside England was also the first to feature 50-overs-a-side matches, the first to have a lunch interval between the two innings and the first to not have a tea interval. It was also the first World Cup to feature an international umpiring panel. The seven Test-playing nations were once again joined by Zimbabwe, winners of the ICC Trophy in 1986. Matches were played across the length and breadth of the subcontinent, from the city of Peshawar, which was close to Pakistan's border with Afghanistan, to the metropolis of Kolkata in eastern India. The co-hosts were the favourites to meet in the final, but they were beaten in the semi-finals by the inventors of the game. The tournament was the last international assignment of Sunil Gavaskar, the first batsman to score 10,000 runs in Test cricket.

FACTFILE: RELIANCE WORLD CUP 1987

Hosts: India and Pakistan
Duration: 8 October–8 November
Participating teams: 8
Matches: 27
Venues: 14 in India and 7 in Pakistan
Title sponsor: Reliance Industries (£2,170,000)

1987: THE START OF THE GLOBAL JOURNEY

Trophy: A gold-plated cup, embellished with diamonds and the flags of the participating nations

Format: The same as in 1983

Prize money: £99,300

Prize money for the winners: £30,000

Groups–

A: India, Australia, New Zealand, Zimbabwe

B: Pakistan, England, West Indies, Sri Lanka

Winners: Australia

Runners-up: England

Losing semi-finalists: Pakistan (beaten by Australia) and India (beaten by England)

Highest scorer: Graham Gooch (England)—478 runs @58.8 from eight matches, inclusive of a century and 3 fifties

Gooch's highest score: 115 v India at Wankhede Stadium, Mumbai (semi-final)

Highest wicket-taker: Craig McDermott (Australia)—18 wickets @18.9 from eight matches, inclusive of one 5-wicket haul

McDermott's best bowling figures: 5/44 v Pakistan at Gaddafi Stadium, Lahore (semi-final)

THE TRAIL OF CRICKET'S HOLY GRAIL

CLASSIC CLASHES

Group A: Australia v India, M.A. Chidambaram Stadium, Chennai, 9 October 1987

Put in to bat by the defending champions, Australia were given a sound start by David Boon and Geoffrey Marsh. The latter went on to score a century. Dean Jones, No. 3, also had a good outing. A lofted hit by him off Maninder Singh was declared a six, but 2 runs were deducted when the Indians claimed that the ball had landed short of the boundary. The runs were restored to the score at the end of the innings after a discussion between the match adjudicator, the Australian manager and the Indian captain. India got off to a rollicking start. Sunil Gavaskar outshone K. Srikkanth, his pugnacious partner, in an opening stand that ended with the little master's dismissal for 37. Srikkanth went on to score 70, and Navjot Sidhu, playing his first international match after four years, impressed watchers with a fine innings. With 63 needed from 78 balls and 8 wickets in hand, the Indians were cruising, but Craig McDermott, the leader of Australia's bowling attack, initiated a collapse. The Indians added to their woes with 2 run outs. Steve Waugh, who relished bowling at the death, was entrusted with the job of preventing the Indians from scoring 6 runs in the final over. Maninder, India's No. 11, managed 4 runs off the first 4 balls, but was comprehensively bowled off the fifth. The 2 runs that were added to Australia's score at the interval made all the difference.

Result: Australia [270/6 (50)] beat India [269 (49.5)] by 1 run.

Group B: Pakistan v West Indies, Gaddafi Stadium, Lahore, 16 October 1987

Group B was the 'Group of Death', with the West Indies, England and Pakistan vying for two semi-final spots. Needing 217 to win their first group match against the two-time champions, Pakistan benefited from lapses in the field to come within striking distance. However, Courtney Walsh and Patrick Patterson choked the scoring in the 48th and 49th overs respectively, leaving Pakistan's last pair with 14 to get from the final over. Abdul Qadir and Salim Jaffer took singles off Walsh's first 2 balls and capitalized on an overthrow to complete a 2 off the third. 10 were needed off 3. What happened next was incredible; Qadir backed away to the leg side and hoisted one of the fastest bowlers in the world for a six over long off. Another improvised stroke yielded 2 runs off the next ball. Walsh ran in to bowl the final delivery and stopped just as he neared the wickets; Jaffer, the non-striker, had backed up too far. Walsh could have followed the letter of the law and run the batsman out to win the match for his team, but he opted to follow the spirit of the law instead and merely issued a warning. He ran in again, aiming to bowl a yorker, but it ended up being a full toss that Qadir steered to third man for 2 runs, to win the match. This defeat would eventually cost the West Indies a semi-final spot for the first time since the inception of the tournament.

Result: West Indies [216 (49.3)] lost to Pakistan [217/9 (50)] by 1 wicket.

First semi-final: Australia v Pakistan, Gaddafi Stadium, Lahore, 4 November 1987

The Australians, who had finished second in Group A, were the overwhelming underdogs on the eve of their 'final four' clash against the Group B topper on the latter's home turf. Allan Border was happy to win the toss and bat, considering that his team had batted first in all the matches that it had won in the competition. Openers Boon and Marsh put on 73 and Dean Jones also looked good until he and Boon fell at the same score. Border, always at his best when the opposing side had its tail up, added 60 with Mike Veletta before being run out. Veletta was bowled by Imran soon after, and Pakistan appeared to have regained the initiative when a misunderstanding between Steve Waugh and Simon O'Donnell resulted in both of them finishing up at the same end. Waugh assumed that he was out, but he was recalled by the umpires, who adjudged his partner out instead. The all-rounder made the most of this reprieve with an enterprising innings, which included 18 runs off the last over, bowled by Salim Jaffer. Pakistan began their chase of 268 disastrously, losing 3 quick wickets. Imran and Miandad added 112, but they were not allowed to settle down. The Australians ensured that the required rate continued to climb, and kept chipping away. Craig McDermott took 5 wickets and the co-hosts were dismissed for 249. The 18 runs scored by Waugh in the last over of the Australian innings proved to be critical.

Result: Australia [267/8 (50)] beat Pakistan [249 (49)] by 18 runs.

Second semi-final: England v India, Wankhede Stadium, Mumbai, 5 November 1987

Kapil Dev won the toss and elected to bowl. Any hopes that he, his team and the capacity crowd may have entertained of restricting England to a modest score were swept away by Graham Gooch, quite literally. The English opener countered the left-arm spin of Maninder Singh and Ravi Shastri brilliantly after having practised the sweep shot for hours on the eve of the game. Gooch scored 115. Mike Gatting, the England captain, scored 56 and Allan Lamb went for the runs in the closing overs. Needing 255 to win, India lost Gavaskar with only 7 on the board. Srikkanth, Sidhu and Chandrakant

THE TRAIL OF CRICKET'S HOLY GRAIL

Pandit got off to starts, but could not consolidate. Kapil Dev came in at 121/4 and sought to turn the match his team's way with some big hits. With Mohammed Azharuddin playing well at the other end, India were very much in the game until the captain had a rush of blood after lofting Eddie Hemmings, the off spinner, to the mid-wicket boundary. He repeated the stroke off the very next ball but was caught by Gatting. Azharuddin carried on until he fell leg before to Hemmings for 64. The score at that stage was 204/6 and the target still gettable, but the last 4 wickets fell for 15 runs. The fact that there were more than 4 overs left in the Indian innings when Shastri was the last man out suggested that the outcome could well have been different had the Indians applied themselves a little bit more.

Result: England [254/6 (50)] beat India [219 (45.3)] by 35 runs.

Final: Australia v England, Eden Gardens, Kolkata, 8 November 1987

The Australians were 'adopted' by the full house at the expense of England, the erstwhile 'rulers'. Border won the toss and followed his favoured practice of batting first. Australia scored 253/5, with David Boon top-scoring with 75. England lost Tim Robinson early. Gooch's dismissal at 66 brought Mike Gatting to the crease. The England captain proceeded to bat beautifully. England needed 119 to win from 114 balls, with

1987: THE START OF THE GLOBAL JOURNEY

their skipper and Bill Athey in fine nick, when the Australian captain decided to bowl. Border's first ball landed well outside the leg stump, but instead of playing it on the leg side, Gatting decided to improvise. He brought out the reverse sweep from his repertoire, but unfortunately for him and England, the ball took the top edge of his bat and hit him on his right shoulder, off which it ricocheted and ballooned into the air. Greg Dyer, Australia's wicketkeeper, made no mistake. Athey added 33 with Allan Lamb before he took on Steve Waugh's throwing arm and was run out attempting a third run. His 58 turned out to be the highest individual score of England's innings. Allan Lamb scored 45 before he was bowled by Waugh, who once again displayed his 'nerves of steel' at the death. Phillip DeFreitas launched a late assault, but Waugh came to Australia's rescue, conceding only 2 runs in the 49th over and most importantly, having DeFreitas caught in the deep. McDermott began the final over with England needing 17 to win. He conceded only 9.

Result: Australia [253/5 (50)] beat England [246/8 (50)] by 7 runs.

THE 1987 WORLD CUP QUIZ

1. Name the venue that hosted the first World Cup match to be played on the Indian subcontinent.

THE TRAIL OF CRICKET'S HOLY GRAIL

2. Ken Rutherford and Ewen Chatfield were Chetan Sharma's first and third victims respectively when he completed the hat trick in a league match against New Zealand. Name the second.
3. Who broke Kapil Dev's 1983 record for the highest individual score in a World Cup match, in the 1987 edition?
4. India's Ram Babu Gupta was one of the two umpires who stood in the final. Name the other.
5. Ten batsmen scored centuries in the competition. One of them scored 2. Name him.
6. The only match Australia lost in the tournament was the only one in which they batted second. Who scored an unbeaten half century and took 3 wickets in the match?
7. Who captained Zimbabwe in the tournament?
8. I played in the 1983 and 1987 World Cups. I was my father's namesake. Another namesake of mine lost a final at Wimbledon in the mid-1980s. Two of my sons are Test cricketers. Who am I?
9. I played the first four World Cups and scored my only ODI hundred in the 1987 edition in what was the penultimate match of my international career. Who am I?
10. Who was India's highest wicket-taker in the competition?

1987: THE START OF THE GLOBAL JOURNEY

THE 1987 WORLD CUP QUIZ: ANSWERS

1. The first match of the 1987 World Cup was played between Pakistan and Sri Lanka at the Niaz Stadium, Hyderabad (Pakistan) on 8 October 1987.
2. Ian Smith
3. Vivian Richards' 181 against Sri Lanka at the National Stadium, Karachi, was the highest individual score in the World Cup till 1996.
4. Mahboob Shah (Pakistan)
5. Geoff Marsh (Australia) scored 110 against India and an unbeaten 126 against New Zealand at Chennai and Chandigarh respectively.
6. Mohammed Azharuddin starred with bat and ball in India's second league match against Australia, which was played at Delhi. He scored an unbeaten 54 and then took 3/19.
7. John Traicos
8. Kevin Curran (Zimbabwe). Tom and Sam, two of his sons, have represented England in Tests. Kevin shared his name with his father, who was a first class cricketer. Kevin Curren, another namesake, was a tennis player who lost to Boris Becker in the Men's Singles final at Wimbledon in 1985.

THE TRAIL OF CRICKET'S HOLY GRAIL

9. Sunil Gavaskar scored an unbeaten 103 against New Zealand at the VCA Stadium (old), Nagpur.
10. Maninder Singh took 14 wickets in the tournament.

5

1992: CORNERED TIGERS

THE FIFTH WORLD Cup was the first in an even-numbered year, played as it was at the end of the season in Australia and New Zealand. It was the first World Cup to feature coloured clothing, white balls, black sight screens and of course, floodlights. It was also the first without groups and with nine participants. South Africa, who returned to international cricket in 1991 after a twenty-one-year embargo, made their debut in the competition. The debutants qualified for the semi-finals, but Australia, the defending champions, flopped. A discordant note was struck by Rule 5.2 of the Playing Conditions, which stated that if circumstances necessitated a reduction in the number of overs available to the chasing side, then the revised target would be computed by not considering the runs scored in the corresponding number of 'lowest-scoring' overs in the first innings. The rule was invoked in rain-affected matches with acrimonious results, like in the second semi-final between England and South Africa. South Africa, who bowled only 45 overs in the allotted time, needed 253 to win. The equation was down to 22 runs from 13 balls when it started raining. Rule 5.2 came into play and 2 overs were deducted from South Africa's innings. Accordingly, the 2 'lowest-scoring' overs of England's innings—2 maidens—were 'not considered'. The consequence—South Africa's score was revised to 22 from 1 ball. Imran Khan's 'cornered tigers', who were at one point close to an ignominious exit, peaked at the right time. Zimbabwe qualified for the tournament for the third consecutive time with their victory in the ICC Trophy in 1990.

FACTFILE: BENSON AND HEDGES WORLD CUP 1992

Hosts: Australia and New Zealand

Duration: 22 February–25 March

Teams: 9

Matches: 39

Venues: 11 in Australia and 7 in New Zealand

1992: CORNERED TIGERS

Title sponsor: Benson and Hedges (£3,000,000)

Trophy: Waterford crystal globe

Format: The nine teams—eight Test-playing teams and Zimbabwe—played each other once in a round-robin league. The top four teams qualified for the semi-finals.

Prize money: £118,000

Prize money for the winners: £20,500

Winners: Pakistan

Runners-up: England

Losing semi-finalists: New Zealand (beaten by Pakistan) and South Africa (beaten by England)

Highest scorer: Martin Crowe (New Zealand)—456 runs @114 from nine matches, inclusive of a century and 4 fifties

Crowe's highest score: 100* v Australia at Eden Park, Auckland

Highest wicket-taker: Wasim Akram (Pakistan)—18 wickets @18.7 from ten matches

Akram's best bowling figures: 4/32 v New Zealand at Lancaster Park, Christchurch

Player of the tournament: Martin Crowe

CLASSIC CLASHES

New Zealand v Australia, Eden Park, Auckland, 22 February 1992

Australia went into the opening match of the fifth World Cup as the overwhelming favourites to win not only the match, but also the competition itself. Martin Crowe, the New Zealand captain, won the toss and led from the front. He scored an unbeaten century and his team totalled 248/6. The most radical tactic in the history of ODI cricket (until that point) was unveiled in the second over of Australia's innings. The cricketing world, used to seeing two pacemen open the proceedings, was incredulous when Dipak Patel, the off spinner, was handed the ball. He did an incredible job, conceding only 19 from his first 7 overs, all of them bowled when the field restrictions were in place, with only two men standing outside the 30-yard circle. Another tactic that took the Australians by surprise was the rapid rotation of the bowlers. Willie Watson, Rod Latham, Gavin Larsen and Chris Harris operated at different speeds, but what all of them had in common was cricketing parsimony. The combination of accurate bowling and splendid fielding nonplussed the batsmen. Australia struggled in the battle of wits, but then, subsequent events proved that they were not alone. Not many teams got the better of New Zealand cerebrally, in the days that followed.

1992: CORNERED TIGERS

David Boon completed a century, but he kept losing partners and was finally run out. Much to the delight of a capacity crowd armed with ear-piercing 'hooters', the Kiwis won by 37 runs.

Result: New Zealand [248/6 (50)] beat Australia [211 (48.1)] by 37 runs.

Zimbabwe v England, Lavington Sports Ground, Albury, 18 March, 1992

After five wins and one 'no result' in a match against Pakistan that they would have won but for the rain, England ruined their cent per cent record with a 7-wicket loss to New Zealand. Graham Gooch's team was keen to return to winning ways in its last league match before taking on South Africa in the semis. The England dressing-room wore a relaxed look at the halfway stage after Zimbabwe, who were asked to bat, were bowled out for 134. England supporters, looking forward to their team finishing the match early, were stunned when Gooch fell leg before to Eddo Brandes off the first ball of the innings. Ian Botham and Allan Lamb took the score to 32 before Brandes had Lamb caught. The paceman was far from done. After his teammate Ali Shah had accounted for Botham, Brandes dismissed Robin Smith and Graeme Hick to reduce England to 43/5. Neil Fairbrother and Alec Stewart steadied the boat with a stand of 52 before the Zimbabwean bowlers and fielders combined to initiate another collapse. This time around, there was no recovery. Fairbrother was the eighth one out at 108 when he nicked Ian Butchart to the keeper. England needed 10 off the last over, with the last pair at the crease. Gladstone Small hit Malcolm Jarvis' first ball straight down the throat of Andy Pycroft to give Zimbabwe their first ODI win since 9 June 1983. A few months later, the African nation became the ninth full member of the ICC.

Result: Zimbabwe [134 (46.1)] beat England [125 (49.1)] by 9 runs.

First semi-final: Pakistan v New Zealand, Eden Park, Auckland, 21 March, 1992

Mark Greatbatch, whose explosive batting at the top of the order had been a highlight of the tournament, fell early after Martin Crowe won the toss and elected to bat. At 87/3, Crowe and Andrew Jones got together for a stand that put their team in command. The New Zealand captain was outstanding and he would probably have scored a century had his hamstring not acted up. With the target a stiff 263, Imran Khan promoted himself to No. 3 to monitor the chase, but the Kiwis were miserly with the ball. The fourth wicket fell at 140 and with 123 more to get in 92 balls, the co-hosts held all the aces. Imran, who had fallen by then, sent

1992: CORNERED TIGERS

in Inzamam-ul-Haq, a gawky teenager from Multan. The youngster, who owed his place in the squad to his captain's penchant for spotting talent, proceeded to blast 60 off 37 balls. Among those taken aback by the assault were New Zealand's medium pacers, who had exasperated batsmen right through the tournament with their nagging line and length. When Inzamam was run out, 36 were needed off 32 balls. Javed Miandad, who had kept things going at the other end, then brought all his experience into play. 9 were needed off 8 balls when Moin Khan swung Gavin Larsen with a horizontal bat over long off for a six. He pulled the next delivery for a boundary to take his team into a World Cup final for the first time ever.

Result: New Zealand [262/7 (50)] lost to Pakistan [264/6 (49)] by 4 wickets.

Final: Pakistan v England, Melbourne Cricket Ground, 25 March, 1992

Pakistan lost both openers shortly after Imran Khan won the toss and opted to bat. The legendary duo of Imran and Miandad then dropped anchor. Their teammates were more than a little concerned when the innings reached triple figures only in the 31st over. However, the veterans knew exactly what they were doing. They proceeded to accelerate and then left it to Inzamam and Wasim Akram to explode at the death. England were set a round 250 to win. Akram had Botham caught behind with only 6 runs on the board and Alec Stewart fell in the same fashion to Aaqib Javed. England fared no better against spin. Mushtaq Ahmed, the leggie, deceived Graeme Hick with a googly and had Gooch superbly caught by Aaqib in the deep. Allan Lamb and Neil Fairbrother commenced the rebuilding operation at 69/4. Akram returned for another spell just when it seemed that the chase was back on track. The left-armer bowled 4 balls before deciding to go around the wicket. His first 2 deliveries from that approach rank among the best deliveries of all time; the first one, angled into Lamb, straightened after pitching and took the off stump, and the second went the other way to pierce the defence of Chris Lewis. The match ended as a contest for all practical purposes at that point, although Fairbrother fought valiantly. Fittingly, Imran Khan, the charismatic captain of a magnificent team, took the final wicket in what was the final international match of his career.

Result: Pakistan [249/6 (50)] beat England [227 (49.2)] by 22 runs.

THE 1992 WORLD CUP QUIZ

1. A certain cricketer made his international debut in what was my 109th Test. Nearly twenty-one years after that

1992: CORNERED TIGERS

match, I presented the same cricketer with the World Cup. Who am I?

2. Martin Crowe, the New Zealand captain, pulled his hamstring while batting in the semi-final against Pakistan and could not take the field as a result. Who led New Zealand in his absence during Pakistan's innings?
3. I played in the 1992 World Cup. My son, who was born a few days after the conclusion of the tournament, emulated me by representing our country. He is a wicketkeeper-batsman who made his ODI debut in 2012 and Test debut in 2014. Who am I?
4. Who took 4/31 and scored 53 in a league match of the competition?
5. Who led Sri Lanka in the tournament?
6. Who opened the batting with K. Srikkanth in India's league matches against Sri Lanka and Zimbabwe?
7. Who in 1992 became the first—and till date, the only—cricketer to appear in three World Cup finals and lose all three?
8. Fill in the blank: Clive Lloyd, Vivian Richards, Mohinder Amarnath, David Boon, _____.
9. What was significant about the league match between Sri Lanka and Zimbabwe at New Plymouth?
10. With Ian Healy absent due to injury, who kept wickets for Australia in the league match against India?

THE TRAIL OF CRICKET'S HOLY GRAIL

THE 1992 WORLD CUP QUIZ: ANSWERS

1. Sir Colin Cowdrey's 109th Test, against Pakistan at Birmingham in June 1971, was Imran Khan's first. On 25 March 1992, Cowdrey, in his capacity as President of the ICC, presented Imran the World Cup at the presentation ceremony after the final.
2. John Wright
3. Rod Latham represented New Zealand in the 1992 World Cup. Tom Latham, his son, made his ODI debut and Test debut for New Zealand in 2012 and 2014 respectively.
4. Sir Ian Botham. He had an outstanding match with ball and bat against Australia at Sydney.
5. Aravinda de Silva
6. Kapil Dev
7. Graham Gooch (1979, 1987 and 1992)
8. Wasim Akram. He was declared the Player of the 1992 World Cup final.
9. It was the first instance in ODIs of a team (Sri Lanka) successfully chasing a target in excess of 300.
10. David Boon

6

1996: THE PRIDE OF LANKAN LIONS

INDIA, PAKISTAN AND Sri Lanka won the hosting rights of the sixth World Cup in February 1993, in an acrimonious ICC meeting that lasted nearly fourteen hours. The PILCOM (Pakistan, India, Lanka Committee) worked tirelessly to make the tournament a blockbuster well before the first ball was evenbowled. Sponsorship opportunities were created and marketed in just about every aspect of the tournament, from advertising to beverages to hospitality. For the first time, the World Cup featured as many as three associate member-nations. The United Arab Emirates, Kenya and the Netherlands, the winners, runners-up and third-ranked team respectively in the

1994 ICC Trophy, qualified. The group format returned and quarter-finals made their debut appearance in a cricket World Cup. A suicide bombing in Colombo a fortnight before the start of the tournament prompted Australia and the West Indies to refuse to travel to Sri Lanka to play their league matches. Arjuna Ranatunga's side was awarded full points for both matches, as a result. The co-hosts went the distance, becoming the third Asian nation to win the title. Sachin Tendulkar, playing in his second World Cup, became the first batsman to score over 500 runs in a World Cup. The semi-final between India and Sri Lanka at Kolkata made news for all the wrong reasons; India were tottering at 120/8 in response to Sri Lanka's 251/6 when the spectators started hurling rubbish on the ground and the match was awarded to the Sri Lankans by default. Kenya pulled off the upset of the tournament, beating the West Indies in a Group A match on Leap Year day.

FACTFILE: WILLS WORLD CUP 1996

Hosts: India, Pakistan and Sri Lanka

Duration: 14 February–17 March

Participating teams: 12

Matches: 37

Venues: 17 in India, 6 in Pakistan and 3 in Sri Lanka

1996: THE PRIDE OF LANKAN LIONS

Title sponsor: Wills (£8,000,000)

Trophy: A century-old sterling silver trophy, 70 cm in height

Format: Twelve teams were divided into two groups of six each. Each team played the other five in its group once. The top four teams from each group qualified for the quarter-finals.

Mascot: Googlee, an animated cricket ball

Prize money: £200,000

Prize money for the winners: £30,000

Groups –

A: **Sri Lanka, Australia, India, West Indies**, Zimbabwe, Kenya

B: **South Africa, Pakistan, New Zealand, England**, United Arab Emirates, Netherlands

Winners: Sri Lanka

Runners-up: Australia

Losing semi-finalists: India (beaten by Sri Lanka) and West Indies (beaten by Australia)

Highest scorer: Sachin Tendulkar (India)—523 runs @87.1 from seven matches, inclusive of 2 centuries and 3 fifties

Tendulkar's highest score: 137 v Sri Lanka at Delhi

Highest wicket-taker: Anil Kumble (India)—15 wickets @18.7 from seven matches

Kumble's best bowling figures: 3/28 v Kenya at Cuttack

Player of the tournament: Sanath Jayasuriya (Sri Lanka)

CLASSIC CLASHES

Group A: Sri Lanka v India, Feroz Shah Kotla Ground, New Delhi, 2 March 1996

Arjuna Ranatunga won the toss and opted to chase. Sachin Tendulkar led the charge for India with a magnificent innings. He scored 137 and India finished with 271/3. The smiles on Indian faces did not last very long. Sanath Jayasuriya and Romesh Kaluwitharana, their openers, were at their brutal best. If Dipak Patel's taking the new ball had been the tactic of the previous World Cup, then Sri Lanka's game plan of going for broke from ball one was a revelation in the sixth World Cup. It was by no means the first instance of big hitting at the start of an innings, but what was unprecedented was the attack from both ends, which was in stark contrast to the old stratagem of one opener going flat out and the other playing an anchoring role. Sri Lanka's objective was to achieve a score of 100 in the first 15 overs. Not only did they have batsmen capable of tearing a bowling attack apart, but they also had individuals who possessed the temperament and technique to put the shutters down in the event of a collapse. Manoj Prabhakar went for 11 in his first

1996: THE PRIDE OF LANKAN LIONS

over and 22 in his second. The Lankans were 117/1 at the end of the 15th over. Although India subsequently struck thrice in succession, the Sri Lankans were not flustered. Ranatunga and Hashan Tillakaratne strolled to the target figuratively, and at times, literally. They had all the time to do so, thanks to the belligerence of their top order.

Result: India [271/3 (50)] lost to Sri Lanka [272/4 (48.4)] by 6 wickets.

Fourth quarter-final: Australia v New Zealand, M.A. Chidambaram Stadium, Chennai, 11 March 1996

The Australians planned elaborately for Stephen Fleming, Nathan Astle and Chris Cairns on the eve of the match. As it turned out, two batsmen whom they hadn't discussed as extensively put them to the sword in the quarter-final. Lee Germon, the New Zealand captain, won the toss and elected to bat. He scored 89 and added 168 for the fourth wicket with Chris Harris, who batted superbly to score 130. A score of over 300 seemed a foregone conclusion at one stage, but the Australians managed to pull things back in the end overs. The Kiwis finished with 286/8, at that stage, their highest ODI total against their Trans-Tasman rivals. Back in the middle, this time as the wicketkeeper, Germon did an encore of 1992 by throwing the new ball to Dipak Patel. Australia started well and lost their second wicket at 84 when Shane Warne came in to boost the run rate. He did his job to perfection in a cameo of 24. Steve Waugh took his place and a splendid partnership ensued between the twins. Mark Waugh, who had been in imperious nick at the group stage, did not let an attack of cramps get in the way of his elegant stroke play and brisk running between the wickets. His 110 comprised only 6 fours and 2 sixes, but he still scored his runs at nearly a run-a-ball. Steve Waugh completed the chase with more than 2 overs to spare, with Stuart Law at the other end.

Result: New Zealand [286/9 (50)] lost to Australia [289/4 (47.5)] by 6 wickets.

Second semi-final: Australia v West Indies, PCA Stadium, Mohali, 14 March 1996

Mark Taylor's decision to bat on a greenish strip backfired big-time. Curtly Ambrose and Ian Bishop reduced the Australians to 15/4 before anybody realized it. Michael Bevan and Stuart Law, who was lucky to be caught off a no-ball, ensured that the score went past 200. Shivnarine Chanderpaul, who opened for the West Indies, added 68 for the second wicket with Brian Lara and carried on after the latter's dismissal, with Richie Richardson, his captain, for company. The Windies needed only 43 to win in 53 balls with 8 wickets in hand, when

1996: THE PRIDE OF LANKAN LIONS

Chanderpaul was caught by Fleming off McGrath for 80. His dismissal triggered a series of daft moves. Roger Harper and Otis Gibson, both of whom were promoted at the expense of specialist bats Jimmy Adams and Keith Arthurton, perished in quick succession. Adams then fell leg before to Shane Warne, Arthurton was caught behind and Warne won another leg before appeal against Bishop in the penultimate over. The Windies needed 10 off the final over. Richardson pulled the first ball for a four, but he then went for a non-existent single and ran Ambrose out. The West Indies were 9 down, and most critically, Richardson was now at the non-striker's end. Courtney Walsh was bowled first ball. This meant that the West Indies had lost their last 8 wickets for 37 runs. Harry Houdini, the illusionist known for his 'escape' acts, would have been proud of what the Australians had achieved.

Result: Australia [207/8 (50)] beat West Indies [202 (49.3)] by 5 runs.

Final: Sri Lanka v Australia, Gaddafi Stadium, Lahore, 17 March 1996

No team had won a World Cup final batting second. However, the Sri Lankans were happier chasing than defending, and Arjuna Ranatunga acted accordingly when he won the toss. Australia were assertive at the start, but they were frustrated by Sri Lanka's slow bowlers. Mark Taylor and Ricky Ponting, who appeared to have got a partnership going, fell to the off breaks of Aravinda de Silva, Sri Lanka's vice-captain. Like de Silva, the other slow bowlers in Sri Lanka's line-up were also in top form. Muttiah Muralitharan, Kumar Dharmasena and Sanath Jayasuriya prevented the Australians from crossing 250. Sri Lanka started their chase of 242 disastrously, losing their openers with only 23 on the board. Enter Aravinda de Silva, who had scored a stunning 66 off 47 balls against India at Kolkata in the semi-final. He did an encore at Lahore. The left-handed Asanka Gurusinha, Sri Lanka's No. 3, was no less effective. When he fell with 95 still needed, Arjuna Ranatunga came in and set out to finish the match in the company of his deputy. The Australians, Shane Warne in particular, were hampered by the dew on the turf, which made it difficult for them to grip the ball. Aravinda de Silva completed his hundred in the 46th over and the captain gave his team the trophy with a glided boundary to the third man fence in the next over. It was the first successful chase in a World Cup final; the Sri Lankans had looked history in the eye and made it blink.

Result: Australia [241/7 (50)] lost to Sri Lanka [245/3 (46.2)] by 7 wickets.

1996: THE PRIDE OF LANKAN LIONS

THE 1996 WORLD CUP QUIZ

1. The outcome of the semi-final between Australia and the West Indies might have been different had an umpire inadvertently not come in the way of a stroke played by a batsman. The umpire was hit on the head and the West Indies got 2 runs instead of a possible boundary. Name the umpire and the batsman who struck him.
2. Who scored a match-winning hundred in the first match of the tournament?
3. Sachin Tendulkar apart, which Indian scored a century in the tournament?
4. Against which team did Sri Lanka score 398/5, at that point the highest score in ODIs?
5. At which venue did South Africa lose their only match of the tournament?
6. Who made the headlines for batting without a helmet against Allan Donald and getting hit on the head by the bowler?
7. Who made his ODI debut at the age of 47 in the tournament?
8. Name the two batsmen who fell in the first over of the semi-final between India and Sri Lanka.
9. What distinction did Mark Waugh achieve with his centuries against Kenya and India at the group stage?

10. Who in 1996 became the first cricketer to play in six World Cups?

THE 1996 WORLD CUP QUIZ—ANSWERS

1. B.C. Cooray (Sri Lanka) could not get out of the way of a sweep stroke essayed by Richie Richardson off Shane Warne and was hit on the head.
2. Nathan Astle of New Zealand scored 101 against England at Ahmedabad on 14 February 1996.
3. Vinod Kambli scored 106 in the group match against Zimbabwe. Tendulkar scored a century each in the group encounters against Kenya and Sri Lanka.
4. Kenya
5. South Africa won all five league matches, but were eliminated from the tournament after losing to the West Indies by 19 runs in the quarter-final at the National Stadium, Karachi.
6. Sultan Zarawani (UAE)
7. Nolan Clarke (the Netherlands)
8. Sanath Jayasuriya and Romesh Kaluwitharana
9. He became the first batsman to score centuries in two consecutive World Cup matches. His 110 against New Zealand in the quarter-final was his third hundred of the tournament.
10. Javed Miandad

7

1999: A TALE OF SEVEN 'FINALS'

AFTER THE INDIAN subcontinent bagged the sixth World Cup hosting rights, the ICC decided to rotate the tournament between member-nations from 1999 to 2007. Had it been left to bids, the Indian subcontinent with its financial muscle would have bagged the hosting rights every time. The seventh World Cup was scheduled a little over three years after the previous edition, in an attempt to restore the four-year cycle that had started in 1975 and been disturbed when the fifth edition was held in 1992 instead of 1991. The seventh World Cup, and fourth to be played in England, was also the first quadrennial tournament that did not have a title sponsor, as the ICC took a cue from its football counterpart. The competition featured two debutants—Bangladesh and Scotland, winners and third-ranked team in the 1997 ICC Trophy respectively. Kenya, runners-up in the same tournament, also qualified. The ICC Cricket World Cup, 1999, as it was called, witnessed one of the greatest resurgences in cricketing history. After losing two of their first three league matches, Australia found themselves in a situation wherein every subsequent match became a 'knockout' encounter—a veritable final—as far as they were concerned. Later in the tournament, they copped criticism for stretching one of the tournament's rules to the extreme; a team that qualified for the 'Super Six' could carry forward the points that it had bagged for winning its league match/matches against the other team/teams that had also qualified from its group. Needing only 111 to beat the West Indies, Australia deliberately went slow to concoct a scenario in which the West Indies would qualify for the Super Six at the expense of New Zealand. The attempt went in vain. New Zealand and Pakistan, both of whom had beaten Australia at the group stage, qualified for the Super Six from Group B, and Australia thus went into the second stage without any points to carry forward. Steve Waugh's team did rather well despite that handicap.

1999: A TALE OF SEVEN 'FINALS'

FACTFILE: ICC CRICKET WORLD CUP 1999

Hosts: England, Scotland, Ireland, Wales and the Netherlands

Duration: 14 May–20 June

Participating teams: 12

Matches: 42

Venues: 17 in England and 1 each in Scotland, Ireland, Wales and the Netherlands

Trophy: A cup that comprised a golden globe, held by three silver columns. The trophy was 60 cm high and 11 kg in weight.

Format: The teams were divided into two groups of six each. Each team played the other five in its group in a round-robin league. The top three teams from each group qualified for the Super Six, where a team from one group played each of the three teams that had qualified from the other group. The top four teams in terms of points at the end of the Super Six made it to the semi-finals.

Prize money: US$ 1,000,000

Prize money for the winners: US$ 300,000

Groups –

A: **South Africa, India, Zimbabwe**, England, Sri Lanka, Kenya

B: **Pakistan, Australia, New Zealand**, West Indies, Bangladesh, Scotland

THE TRAIL OF CRICKET'S HOLY GRAIL

Winners: Australia

Runners-up: Pakistan

Losing semi-finalists: South Africa (their semi-final was tied, but Australia went through to the final because they had beaten South Africa earlier in the competition) and New Zealand (beaten by Pakistan)

Highest scorer: Rahul Dravid (India)—461 runs @65.8 from eight matches, inclusive of 2 centuries and 3 fifties

Dravid's highest score: 145 v Sri Lanka at Taunton

Highest wicket-takers:

Shane Warne (Australia)—20 wickets @18.05 from ten matches

Warne's best bowling figures: 4/29 v South Africa at Birmingham (semi-final)

Geoff Allott (New Zealand)—20 wickets @16.2 from nine matches

Allott's best bowling figures: 4/37 v Australia at Cardiff

Player of the tournament: Lance Klusener (South Africa)

CLASSIC CLASHES

Group B: Pakistan v Australia, Headingley, Leeds, 23 May 1999

Put in to bat, Pakistan lost 3 early wickets before Inzamam-ul-Haq and Abdul Razzaq came together to add 118. Inzamam scored a

1999: A TALE OF SEVEN 'FINALS'

fine 81, unveiling his full repertoire of strokes and piercing the gaps at will, as was his wont. He also betrayed his ineptitude while running between the wickets. Yousuf Youhana had to go after finding himself at the same end as his partner, and then Inzamam himself had to depart after getting into another mix-up with Wasim Akram, his captain. Moin Khan attacked the bowling with gusto at the death. The last 10 overs yielded a sensational 111 runs and Pakistan finished with 275/8. Akram then struck with his third ball, breaching the defence of Adam Gilchrist, Australia's extraordinary keeper-opener, without a run on the board. Mark Waugh and Ponting added 91 before the Pakistanis hit back, reducing the batting side to 101/4. Steve Waugh, the Australian captain, initiated a recovery with Michael Bevan and the duo took the score past 200. The Australians seemed to have got back into the game when Bevan was fifth out at 214. Shoaib Akhtar, the 'Rawalpindi Express', then got the big one. Waugh received a gem of an inswinger that breached his defence and smashed into the stumps. Damien Martyn and the tail took the match into the final over, which began with Australia needing 13. Akram, who had kept the final over for himself, conceded only 2 runs and castled Martyn and McGrath to finish with figures of 4/40.

Result: Pakistan [275/8 (50)] beat Australia [265 (49.5)] by 10 runs.

Group A: Zimbabwe v South Africa, County Ground, Chelmsford, 29 May 1999

South Africa had already qualified for the Super Six when they took on their neighbours in their last Group A match. Alastair Campbell, the Zimbabwe captain, won the toss and elected to bat. His team scored 233/6, with Neil Johnson top-scoring with 76. The third ball of South Africa's innings, bowled by Johnson, took off from a length and Gary Kirsten fended it away for Andy Whittall to take a brilliant catch. The early strike was just the inspiration the Zimbabweans needed. Within minutes, they had South Africa on the mat at 40/6. Daryll Cullinan and Shaun Pollock kept their cool and posted the hundred, but they were made to fight for every run. Lance Klusener came in after Cullinan's dismissal. The left-handed all-rounder threw caution to the wind after Pollock and Steve Elworthy fell in quick succession to reduce the score to 150/9. The overs were running out, but with Klusener striking the ball well and Allan Donald, the No. 11, hanging on, anything was possible. 35 runs were added before Donald allowed the tail-ender in him to come to the fore and swung hard at Henry Olonga. Heath Streak took the catch to confirm Zimbabwe's debut appearance in the second stage of a cricket World Cup. On the other hand, England, who had the same number of points as Zimbabwe before the match, lost their final group match to India and did not make it as a result.

Result: Zimbabwe [233/6 (50)] beat South Africa [185 (47.2)] by 48 runs.

Super Six—Match 9: Australia v South Africa, Headingley, Leeds, 13 June 1999

This was Australia's fifth consecutive 'must-win' match. Their opponents on the other hand had already qualified for the semis. Hansie Cronje won the toss and his team scored 271/7. Herschelle Gibbs, who scored 101, had figured in the pre-match discussions of the Australians for his batting as well as his habit of scooping the ball skywards after taking a catch, thereby giving the impression that he was not in control of the ball. Shane Warne's advice to his teammates to 'not walk immediately' if Gibbs took a catch elicited laughter. Less than twenty-four hours later, Australia were 152/3 in the 31st over and the match was delicately poised when Steve Waugh flicked Klusener to Gibbs, who did exactly what Warne had predicted. Even as Gibbs went for the scoop, the ball slipped out of his palms and fell to the turf. Cronje argued that his fielder had been in control, but the umpires thought otherwise. The Australian captain made the most of the 'life'. The game went down to the wire, with first Michael Bevan and Tom Moody complementing Waugh's efforts. The final over began with Australia needing 8.

Moody scored 2 runs off Shaun Pollock's first ball and pretty much settled the outcome with a boundary off the second. The formalities were then completed and Australia got home with 2 deliveries to spare. Waugh's unbeaten 120 was one of the greatest ODI knocks of all time.

Result: South Africa 271/7 (50) lost to Australia 272/5 (49.4) by 5 wickets.

Second semi-final: Australia v South Africa, Edgbaston, Birmingham, 17 June 1999

Asked to bat first, Australia were dismissed for 213. The South African openers put on 48 before Warne struck thrice. The battle that followed was spectacular. Australia would strike just when South Africa appeared to have regained control. When the ninth wicket fell, the Proteas needed 16 off 8 balls. A dropped catch cost Australia 6 runs and Lance Klusener was on strike with 9 needed when Damien Fleming began bowling the final over. Klusener drilled the first ball to the point fence and biffed the second past extra-cover for another boundary. With the scores level, the Australians crowded the batsmen. Klusener went for a pull off the third ball, but the ball came on to him quicker than he expected. Allan Donald, backing up too far, was nearly run out, with Darren Lehmann's underarm shy missing the stumps by a whisker. Klusener hit the fourth ball straight but not cleanly, and inexplicably took off. Donald wasn't so sure, and he turned

1999: A TALE OF SEVEN 'FINALS'

around to see Mark Waugh fling himself at the ball and throw it back to the bowler. Even as all this was happening, Klusener kept running till he crossed his partner. By the time Donald, horrified at the way things had turned out, had dropped his bat and made for the striker's end, it was too late; Fleming lobbed the ball across the pitch to Adam Gilchrist, who dislodged the bails. The match was tied, but Australia went through because they had beaten South Africa earlier in the tournament.

Result: Australia [213 (49.2)] tied with South Africa [213 (49.4)].

Final: Australia v Pakistan, Lord's, London, 20 June 1999

A lot was expected from the summit clash, which was played three days after the epic at Edgbaston. Wasim Akram won the toss and elected to bat. Pakistan lost their openers early. Abdul Razzaq tried to rally the innings before he was brilliantly caught by Steve Waugh off Moody. The score was 69/3 in 21 overs when Warne, who had taken 4/27 in the semi-final, was introduced into the attack. He initiated a collapse that saw Pakistan slip from 77/3 to 129/9. His second consecutive 4-wicket haul silenced all those who had questioned his presence in the Australian team after an unimpressive tour of the Caribbean, prior to the World Cup. Pakistan were blown away for 132, with 11 overs left. The disappointed Pakistanis were then demoralized by Adam Gilchrist, who launched into the new-ball bowlers as only he could. He completed his 50 off only 33 balls and Mark Waugh, Ricky Ponting and Darren Lehmann did their bit. The match ended in the 21st over. The World Cup final was the seventh consecutive 'final' that the Australians had played after losing their Group B match against Pakistan. They had won six of those and tied one. Steve Waugh was presented the first-ever ICC Cricket World Cup by Jagmohan Dalmiya, who had revitalized the International Cricket Council since the start of his term as its president in 1997. The ICC took full ownership of its biggest event from the next edition in 2003.

Result: Pakistan [132 (39)] lost to Australia [133/2 (20.1)] by 8 wickets.

THE 1999 WORLD CUP QUIZ

1. Who became the first wicketkeeper-batsman after the Zimbabweans Dave Houghton and Andy Flower to score a century in a World Cup match, in the 1999 edition?
2. Who became the second bowler to get a hat trick in a World Cup match during the competition? The first was Chetan Sharma during the 1987 World Cup.
3. Steve Waugh apart, who was the only 'playing' member of the Australian team of 1999 who had also been a part of the 1987 World Cup winning side?

1999: A TALE OF SEVEN 'FINALS'

4. At which venue did Bob Woolmer, the coach of the South African team, communicate with his captain Hansie Cronje and Allan Donald through an earpiece, during a match?
5. What did Shane Warne do that Mohinder Amarnath and Aravinda de Silva had achieved in earlier editions of the World Cup?
6. Four Indians scored centuries in the tournament. Sachin Tendulkar, Sourav Ganguly and Rahul Dravid (with 2 centuries) were three of them. Name the fourth.
7. Against which team did Pakistan suffer its only loss at the group stage?
8. Which was the only match of the competition to be played in the Netherlands?
9. Who returned the best bowling figures of his ODI career in the Group A match between India and Sri Lanka?
10. I was one of the most successful all-rounders of the tournament, with 367 runs and 12 wickets. Who am I?

THE 1999 WORLD CUP QUIZ: ANSWERS

1. Rahul Dravid scored 145 against Sri Lanka at Taunton in a Group A match in which he was India's designated wicketkeeper.
2. Saqlain Mushtaq performed the hat trick in the Super

Six match against Zimbabwe at the Oval, London. He had Henry Olonga and Adam Huckle stumped by Moin Khan and Mpumelelo Mbangwa leg before off the first 3 deliveries of the 41st over.

3. Tom Moody (Geoffrey Marsh, who had been a member of Australia's 1987 team, was coach of the team that won the World Cup in 1999.)
4. At the County Ground, Hove, during the Group A match against India. The ICC subsequently banned the use of earpieces.
5. He won the individual award in the semi-final and final of the tournament. Amarnath and Aravinda de Silva had done likewise in the 1983 and 1996 World Cups respectively.
6. Ajay Jadeja scored an unbeaten century in the Super Six match against Australia at the Oval, London.
7. Bangladesh beat Pakistan by 62 runs in a Group B match at Northampton.
8. The Group A match between South Africa and Kenya at Amstelveen
9. Robin Singh (5/31)
10. Neil Johnson (Zimbabwe)

8

2003: AWESOME AUSSIES—I

SOUTH AFRICA PULLED out all stops to deliver a tournament that would be remembered for years to come. That cricket's ultimate competition was being hosted by a country that till about fifteen years previously had practised racial discrimination marked a triumph of sports over politics. However, the ugly head of politics did rear itself during the tournament; England protested against the breakdown of democratic institutions in Zimbabwe by refusing to play the co-hosts in Harare, and New Zealand did not fly to Nairobi for their Pool B match against Kenya, citing 'security concerns'. As had happened in 1996, full points were awarded to Zimbabwe and Kenya respectively. The latter created history by making it to the semis. The eighth World Cup was the first to feature fourteen teams. Bangladesh had become the 10th Test-playing team in 2000, and Kenya, who had played in the previous two World Cups, had been granted ODI status. Canada, who finished third in the 2001 ICC Trophy, made their first appearance in the World Cup since 1979. The Netherlands, winners of the ICC Trophy, returned after 1996, and Namibia, the runners-up, made their debut. The competition had a Super Six stage like its 1999 predecessor, the difference being that teams that qualified for the second stage carried forward a quarter of the points won by them for beating teams that did not qualify, along with the points bagged by them for beating teams that qualified. Australia bettered their display of 1999 with an extraordinary unbeaten run in the tournament.

FACTFILE: ICC CRICKET WORLD CUP 2003

Hosts: South Africa, Zimbabwe and Kenya

Duration: 9 February–23 March

Participating teams: 14

Matches: 54

Venues: 12 in South Africa, 2 in Zimbabwe and 1 in Kenya

Trophy: The same as in 1999

Format: The fourteen teams were divided into two pools

2003: AWESOME AUSSIES—I

of seven each. Each team played the other six in its group once. The top three teams from each pool qualified for the Super Six.

Mascot: Dazzle, the Zebra

Prize money: US$ 4,500,000

Prize money for the winners: US$ 2,000,000

Groups –

Pool A: **Australia, India, Zimbabwe**, England, Pakistan, Netherlands, Namibia

Pool B: **Sri Lanka, Kenya, New Zealand**, South Africa, West Indies, Canada, Bangladesh

Winners: Australia

Runners-up: India

Losing semi-finalists: Kenya (lost to India) and Sri Lanka (lost to Australia)

Highest scorer: Sachin Tendulkar (India)—673 runs @61.1 from eleven matches, inclusive of a century and 6 fifties

Tendulkar's highest score: 152 v Namibia at Pietermaritzburg

Highest wicket-taker: Chaminda Vaas (Sri Lanka)—23 wickets @14.3, inclusive of one 6-wicket haul

Vaas's best bowling figures: 6/25 v Bangladesh at Pietermaritzburg

Player of the tournament: Sachin Tendulkar (India)

CLASSIC CLASHES

Pool A: Australia v Pakistan, New Wanderers Stadium, Johannesburg, 11 February 2003

Hours before they commenced their defence of the title they had won in 1999, the Australian players learnt that Shane Warne, legend and the hero of their previous triumph, had tested positive for a banned diuretic drug in a test administered by the Australian Sports Drugs Agency a couple of weeks earlier, and was pulling out of the tournament as a result. It was an unexpected cricketing and psychological setback. Things did not look too great on the field either, after Waqar Younis, Pakistan's captain, won the toss and elected to bowl. Australia lost their fourth wicket with only 86 on the board. Andrew Symonds then supported Ricky Ponting, his captain, in a stand of 60. Shoaib Akhtar's dismissal of Ponting for 53 turned out to be Pakistan's last moment of joy in the match as Symonds tore into one of the most formidable bowling line-ups of all time. Brad Hogg and Ian Harvey essayed excellent

2003: AWESOME AUSSIES—I

supporting hands, with Symonds getting a standing ovation for his unbeaten 143. To add insult to injury for the Pakistanis, Waqar was ordered out of the attack for bowling two beamers to Symonds. Set 311 to win, Pakistan were bowled out for 228. Medium pacer Ian Harvey and chinaman (left arm wrist spin) bowler Brad Hogg shared 7 wickets between them. The victory underscored the tenacity and resilience of the Australians. It was obvious that the other thirteen sides would have to do something exceptional to prevent the holders from repeating their feat of 1999.

Result: Australia [310/8 (50)] beat Pakistan [228 (44.3)] by 82 runs.

Pool A: Australia v England, St. George's Park, Port Elizabeth, 2 March 2003

England needed to win this match to finish third in the pool, behind Australia and India. This was easier said than done, considering the way Australia had outplayed their earlier opponents in the competition. Nasser Hussain, the England captain, won the toss and Marcus Trescothick and Nick Knight got their team off to a good start. England were doing well when Ponting brought on Andy Bichel, who was playing in place of the injured Jason Gillespie. The replacement broke the back of the England innings, dismissing Knight, Michael Vaughan, Nasser Hussain, Paul Collingwood, Andrew Flintoff,

Alec Stewart and Ashley Giles. Australia needed only 205 to win, but England took 4 Australian wickets with only 48 on the board, before Darren Lehmann and Michael Bevan dropped anchor. There was another collapse after they were separated, and at 135/8, England had all but got a foot in the Super Six door. However, they were thwarted by Bevan, and the player who had taken 7/20 earlier in the day. It seemed that Andy Bichel was intent on reminding watchers of the adage that the strength of a team was best determined by the quality of its 'bench-strength'. England fought on, but their best wasn't good enough. Bichel sealed the match in his team's favour with a six and a four in the penultimate over, bowled by James Anderson. Bevan hit the winning runs in the last over. The duo had added an undefeated 73 for the ninth wicket.

Result: England [204/8 (50)] lost to Australia [208/8 (49.4)] by 2 wickets.

Pool B: Sri Lanka v South Africa, Kingsmead, Durban, 3 March 2003

South Africa needed to win their last Pool B match to qualify for the Super Six at the expense of either Sri Lanka or Kenya. Sanath Jayasuriya, the Sri Lankan captain, won the toss and elected to bat. A century by Marvan Atapattu and 73 by Aravinda de Silva enabled them to post 268/9. Herschelle Gibbs and Graeme Smith, the South African openers, put on 65

2003: AWESOME AUSSIES—I

before being separated. The Sri Lankan bowlers then dried up the runs, with Jayasuriya himself and Aravinda de Silva bowling excellently. The South African middle order floundered, but the co-hosts were heartened by the purposeful batting of Shaun Pollock and Mark Boucher, their captain and vice-captain respectively. Pollock's dismissal brought in Lance Klusener, the star of 1999, with his team needing 57 from 45 deliveries. A drizzle intensified into a shower by the time the 45th over got underway. Both teams consulted the Duckworth-Lewis sheets and it was conveyed to the batsmen that they needed to reach 229 by the end of that over. They were 6 runs short, with 2 deliveries left. Boucher hit the first ball for a six and defended the second. It was only after the umpires called for the covers that the South Africans realized that they had bungled. 229 was what they needed to *tie* the match! To win, they needed 1 run more. No further play was possible. The two points that the hosts got for the tie were not enough to take them through to the Super Six.

Result: Sri Lanka [268/9 (50)] tied with South Africa [229/6 (45)] as per the Duckworth-Lewis method.

Super Six—Match 4: India v Sri Lanka, New Wanderers Stadium, Johannesburg, 10 March 2003

India did not get off to the best of starts in the competition, with an unconvincing win in their first match against the Netherlands and then a 9-wicket loss to Australia. The team recovered its bearings in the next match against Zimbabwe and only kept getting better and better as the tournament progressed. The Super Six match against Sri Lanka was the apogee of Sourav Ganguly's side in the competition. The Indians wanted to beat Sri Lanka to enhance its prospects of playing Kenya in the semi-finals. Jayasuriya's decision to bat after winning the toss went against his team. Sachin Tendulkar, who was in tremendous form, put on 153 for the first wicket with Virender Sehwag. The Sri Lankans managed to pull things back and dismissed Tendulkar for 97, but the Indians were able to get close to the 300-run mark. Sri Lanka needed a good start to boost their chances of overhauling the target of 293, but they were rocked by India's pace triumvirate. Javagal Srinath and Zaheer Khan's early burst reduced the opposition to 15/4, with all four batsmen who were dismissed not being allowed to open their respective accounts. Ashish Nehra, who bowled first-change, was as effective. Although Kumara Sangakkara tried to do what he could, the result was a foregone conclusion. The Sri Lankan innings ended at 109 in 23 overs. Ganguly did not need a fourth bowler. Srinath and Nehra bowled 9 and 7 overs respectively for identical figures of 4/35 and Zaheer bowled 7 to take 2/33.

Result: India [292/6 (50)] beat Sri Lanka [109 (23)] by 183 runs.

2003: AWESOME AUSSIES—I

Final: Australia v India, New Wanderers Stadium, Johannesburg, 23 March 2003

The Indians squared off against the only side that had beaten them in the competition, in the summit clash. Weaknesses were conspicuous by their absence in the Australian line-up, which had won ten matches out of ten before the final. India's best chance, according to many, was to bat if they won the toss, and post a challenging score. Ganguly did win the toss, but the damp patches on the pitch, the consequence of an early morning shower, prompted him to put the Australians in to bat. The toss turned out to be India's only success of the day. Zaheer Khan went for 15 in his first over and thereafter, the Indians were only trying to catch up with their opponents. The Australian openers put on 105 and set the stage for Ricky Ponting to essay an exceptional innings. His 140 was the first century by a captain in a World Cup final since Clive Lloyd's 102 in 1975. Damien Martyn scored 88 and Australia closed at a modest 359/2. Tendulkar got off the mark with a boundary in the first over, but fell to a return catch by Glenn McGrath while attempting another. Virender Sehwag got 82 and Rahul Dravid managed 47, but the required rate got the better of the other batsmen. The match ended in the 40th over when Zaheer Khan gave a catch to Darren Lehmann off McGrath. It was Australia's third World Cup triumph, their second on the trot and the most comprehensive of the three.

THE TRAIL OF CRICKET'S HOLY GRAIL

Result: Australia [359/2 (50)] beat India [234 (39.2)] by 125 runs.

THE 2003 WORLD CUP QUIZ

1. My father played three World Cups. I represented my country in four, the 2003 World Cup being the last. Who am I?
2. Name the two players who wore black armbands in a Pool A match to mourn the death of democracy in Zimbabwe.
3. Who took his 500th ODI wicket during the tournament?
4. Name the umpire who was nearly decapitated by a Sachin Tendulkar drive during the match between India and Namibia at Pietermaritzburg.
5. Which team did India, the runners-up, defeat twice in the competition?
6. I took 7/15, the best-ever bowling performance in a World Cup match, in the 2003 edition. I am the most successful bowler in World Cup history with 71 wickets. Who am I?
7. Name the Indian who scored 3 centuries in the tournament.
8. Who performed a hat trick off the first 3 balls of a match in the tournament?

2003: AWESOME AUSSIES—I

9. Two bowlers returned identical figures of 6/23 in separate matches of the competition. One of them was Ashish Nehra, who produced those figures in India's Pool A match against England. Name the other.
10. Who was forced to retire hurt, but returned to the middle to try and win a match for his team?

THE 2003 WORLD CUP QUIZ: ANSWERS

1. Chris Cairns represented New Zealand in the 1992, 1996, 1999 and 2003 World Cups. Lance Cairns, his father, played for New Zealand in the first three World Cups.
2. Andy Flower and Henry Olonga wore black armbands in the Pool A match between Zimbabwe and Namibia at Harare.
3. Wasim Akram became the first bowler in ODI history to take 500 wickets when he dismissed Nick Statham (bowled) in the Pool B match against the Netherlands at Paarl.
4. Aleem Dar
5. Kenya
6. Glenn McGrath took 7/15 against Namibia at Potchefstroom.
7. Sourav Ganguly scored 2 centuries against Kenya (the first in the Super Six game at Cape Town and the second

THE TRAIL OF CRICKET'S HOLY GRAIL

   in the semi-final at Durban) and one in the Pool A match against Namibia at Pietermaritzburg.
8. Chaminda Vaas dismissed Hannan Sarkar (bowled), Mohammad Ashraful (caught and bowled) and Ehsanul Haque (caught by Jayawardene) off the first 3 deliveries of the Pool B match between Sri Lanka and Bangladesh at Pietermaritzburg.
9. Shane Bond (New Zealand) took 6/23 in the Super Six match against Australia at Port Elizabeth.
10. Ramnaresh Sarwan was hit on the head by a Dilhara Fernando bouncer and carried off the field in a crucial Pool B match between the West Indies and Sri Lanka at Cape Town. He returned to the middle with his team needing 60 off 47 balls and joined the attack. His heroics went in vain as Sri Lanka won by 6 runs.

9

2007: AWESOME AUSSIES—II

THE NINTH WORLD Cup and the first to be staged in the Caribbean was the most ambitious ever planned. The number of teams was increased to sixteen, with the ten full members of the ICC and Kenya, who enjoyed ODI status, being joined by Scotland, Canada, the Netherlands, Ireland and Bermuda, the top five sides in the 2005 ICC Trophy. The two-group format that had been seen in every World Cup except the one in 1992 was discarded in 2007. The teams were divided into as many as four groups of four each; every team was to play the other three in its group once, and the top two sides from every group were to qualify for the Super Eights. There were murmurs of discontent in the lead-up to the tournament, with fans complaining about the duration of the tournament and apprehensive about many of the matches being one-sided and meaningless. The authorities did not realize that in reversing what had been done in 1983, there was now a distinct possibility of a leading contender's campaign being jeopardized if it was to lose even a single group match. Unfortunately, that was exactly what happened, with India and Pakistan, two of the tournament's biggest box office attractions, crashing out in the first round itself. The tournament was also afflicted by tragedy. Bob Woolmer, Pakistan's coach, was found dead in his hotel room hours after his team's exit from the tournament. A redeeming feature of the tournament was the performance of Australia. The champions of 1999 and 2003 excelled themselves, literally and figuratively.

FACTFILE: ICC CRICKET WORLD CUP 2007

Hosts: West Indies

Duration: 13 March–28 April

Participating teams: 16

Matches: 51

Venues: 8

Trophy: The same as in 1999 and 2003—a rotating trophy

Format: The sixteen countries were divided into four groups of four teams each. Each team played the other three in its group

2007: AWESOME AUSSIES—II

once. The top two teams from each group qualified for the Super Eights. Each team played the six sides that had qualified from the other three groups in the Super Eights. The top four sides at the end of the Super Eights qualified for the semi-finals.

Mascot: Mello the mongoose

Prize money: US$ 5,000,000

Prize money for the winners: US$ 2,400,000

Groups –

A: **Australia, South Africa**, Netherlands, Scotland

B: **Sri Lanka, Bangladesh,** India, Bermuda

C: **New Zealand, England**, Kenya, Canada

D: **West Indies, Ireland**, Pakistan, Zimbabwe

Winners: Australia

Runners-up: Sri Lanka

Losing semi-finalists: New Zealand (lost to Sri Lanka) and South Africa (lost to Australia)

Highest scorer: Matthew Hayden (Australia)—659 runs @73.2 from eleven matches, inclusive of 3 centuries and a fifty

Hayden's highest score: 158 v West Indies at North Sound

Highest wicket-taker: Glenn McGrath (Australia)—26 wickets @13.7

McGrath's best bowling figures: 3/14 v Scotland at Basseterre

Player of the tournament: Glenn McGrath

CLASSIC CLASHES

Group B: Bangladesh v India, Queen's Park Oval, Port of Spain, 17 March 2007

Rahul Dravid, India's captain, won the toss and elected to bat in the first match of the competition for both teams. Indian supporters, who were pleased to see their side begin its campaign at a venue where their team had done well in the past were in for a shock. Bangladesh bowled and fielded excellently and forced India to bat diffidently. Virender Sehwag, Robin Uthappa and Sachin Tendulkar failed to reach double figures. Sourav Ganguly and Yuvraj Singh added 85, but the innings disintegrated when they were separated. Three members of the lower order were dismissed for ducks and the innings folded up for a disappointing 191. Spinners Mohammed Rafique and Abdur Razzaq took 3 wickets each and Mashrafe Mortaza, the spearhead of Bangladesh's attack, finished with 4/38. India's only hope of victory was to strike early. Although Shahriar Nafees fell with only 24 on the board, Tamim Iqbal, the other opener, took India's new-ball bowlers to the cleaners in an innings of 51.

2007: AWESOME AUSSIES—II

Aftab Ahmed's dismissal brought Shakib Al Hasan to the crease. The all-rounder batted superbly to score 53 in the company of Mushfiqur Rahim, who anchored the chase to perfection. Their fourth-wicket stand of 84 sealed the match in their team's favour and Bangladesh completed a comprehensive win in the penultimate over. Mushfiqur batted through the innings to remain unbeaten on 56. India beat Bermuda in their next match but lost to Sri Lanka, thus crashing out of the tournament.

Result: India [191 (49.3)] lost to Bangladesh [192/5 (48.3)] by 5 wickets.

Group D: Ireland v Pakistan, Sabina Park, Kingston, 17 March 2007

This was the second Group D match for both teams; Pakistan had lost their first match to the West Indies and Ireland's encounter against Zimbabwe had ended in a tie. Trent Johnston, the Irish captain, won the toss and put Pakistan in on a wicket that had something in it for the bowlers. The Pakistani batting was as uninspiring as that of their traditional rivals in Port of Spain on the same day. Only three of the top seven batsmen entered double figures. Imran Nazir displayed aggression in the initial overs and Kamran Akmal did his best to resuscitate the innings, but to no avail. The Irish bowlers were rewarded for sticking to the basics. At the halfway mark, the Pakistanis found themselves contending with the challenge of defending a paltry

132 to prevent an early exit from the World Cup with two defeats in as many matches. Mohammed Sami's opening burst reduced Ireland to 15/2, but Neill O'Brien, the wicketkeeper-batsman, came in and batted confidently. He and his colleagues knew that it was simply a question of batting for their full quota of overs. With less than 3 an over to chase, the required rate was never going to be an issue. Pakistan sensed a chance when O'Brien was the fifth man out at 108 for a splendid 72. However, the other O'Brien—his brother Kevin—held his nerve and finished the match in the company of his captain. Pakistan's World Cup was over. 17 March 2007 was a day of upsets.

Result: Pakistan [132 (45.4)] lost to Ireland [133/7 (41.4)] by 3 wickets.

Final: Australia v Sri Lanka, Kensington Oval, Bridgetown, 28 April 2007

Rain delayed the start and reduced the final to a 38-overs-a-side contest. Batting first, Australia got off to a spectacular start, courtesy Adam Gilchrist, who dominated an opening stand of 172 with Matthew Hayden. The keeper-batsman completed his century off only 72 balls and went on to score 149, an innings that comprised 13 boundaries and 8 sixes. The keeper-batsman revealed later that he had batted with a golf ball in his left batting glove, to improve his control over his bat-swing by keeping the ball between his palm and bat. Sri Lanka began their chase of

2007: AWESOME AUSSIES—II

282 well, but the World Champions ensured that the required rate remained stiff. The score was 149/3 from 24.5 overs when play was suspended due to rain; 2 overs were consequently deducted from Sri Lanka's innings and their target revised to 269. The wickets started falling after the resumption, even as the light deteriorated. Sri Lanka needed an impossible 63 off 3 overs with only 2 wickets in hand when the light was offered to the Sri Lankans. They accepted it. With 20 overs having been bowled in the innings, the Australians started celebrating a treble of consecutive World Cup triumphs, only to be informed that the 3 overs would have to be bowled the next day. The two captains then decided that the Sri Lankans would face 18 balls from Australia's slow bowlers in the twilight. Once that was done, Ricky Ponting's team went into a huddle to celebrate all over again.

Result: Australia [281/4 (38)] beat Sri Lanka [215/8 (36)] by 53 runs as per the Duckworth-Lewis method.

THE 2007 WORLD CUP QUIZ

1. What dubious distinction did Dan van Bunge of the Netherlands incur in the Group A match against South Africa at Basseterre?
2. Who took 4 wickets off consecutive deliveries in a group match?

3. A policeman by profession, I was among those instrumental in my team qualifying for the cricket World Cup for the first time. A catch I took at slip in a Group B match is remembered to this day. Who am I?
4. Who emulated Clive Lloyd by becoming the second captain to lead his team to two World Cup triumphs?
5. I flopped in the 2003 World Cup with only 21 runs in seven innings. I went to the other extreme in 2007, finishing as the second-highest scorer in the competition with an aggregate of 548 runs. Who am I?
6. Who in 2007 became the first umpire to stand in five World Cup finals?
7. Bermuda apart, which team suffered two defeats by a margin of more than 200 runs in the tournament?
8. Name the New Zealand cricketer who added 59 runs for the last wicket with James Franklin in the semi-final against Sri Lanka.
9. Name the Indian player who announced his retirement from ODIs after his team's last match of the tournament.
10. Which player scored what was the 100th century in the World Cup, in the tournament?

THE 2007 WORLD CUP QUIZ: ANSWERS

1. He became the first bowler in ODI history to concede

2007: AWESOME AUSSIES—II

6 sixes in an over. Herschelle Gibbs was the batsman who inflicted the damage.
2. Lasith Malinga took 4 wickets off consecutive deliveries against South Africa in a Super Eight encounter at Providence.
3. Dwayne Leverock's consistency with bat and ball in the Intercontinental Cup and ICC Trophy was a key factor in ensuring that Bermuda made their World Cup debut in 2007. He took a spectacular one-handed catch to dismiss Robin Uthappa off Malachi Jones in the Group B match against India at Port of Spain.
4. Ricky Ponting
5. Mahela Jayawardene
6. Steve Bucknor (West Indies) officiated in all the World Cup finals from 1992 to 2007.
7. The Netherlands lost to South Africa and Australia by 221 runs and 229 runs respectively at Basseterre.
8. Jeetan Patel
9. Anil Kumble
10. Matthew Hayden's 103 against New Zealand at Grenada was the 100th World Cup hundred.

10

2011: DHONI'S DEVILS

THE ICC INVITED bids for the tenth edition of the tournament. Pitted against each other in the race to host the tournament were the Australia-New Zealand combine and the Asian quartet of India, Pakistan, Sri Lanka and Bangladesh. However, the Asians missed the submission deadline of 1 April 2006. Their request for an extension was accepted by the ICC in return for confirming India's participation in the inaugural edition of the ICC World T20, which was scheduled to be held in South Africa in September 2007. Ironically, the last country to confirm its participation in the competition ended up winning it, but that is another story. The subcontinent eventually won the rights to host the 2011 World Cup. Pakistan were to take the lead in coordinating the event, but security concerns and

2011: DHONI'S DEVILS

the terrorist attack on the Sri Lankan team at Lahore in 2009 triggered a change in plan. India assumed the chief coordinator's role, with the matches that were to be played in Pakistan being distributed between the three co-hosts. The two-group format was resurrected, and the number of teams reduced back to fourteen. The Super Sixes and Super Eights were replaced by a quarter-final stage. Ireland, Canada, the Netherlands and Kenya[2], the top four sides in the 2009 ICC CWC Qualifier[3], made it to the tournament. The ICC CWC 2011, as it was called, was hailed as the 'most successful' of all the World Cups till that point. The Indian team became the first in World Cup history to win the title on home turf.

FACTFILE: ICC CRICKET WORLD CUP 2011

Hosts: India, Sri Lanka and Bangladesh
Duration: 19 February–2 April
Participating teams: 14
Matches: 49
Venues: 13 (8 in India, 3 in Sri Lanka, 2 in Bangladesh)
Trophy: Rotating trophy

---

[2]Kenya's ODI status was rescinded in 2009.
[3]The ICC Trophy was renamed the ICC CWC Qualifier.

Format: The fourteen teams were divided into two groups of seven teams each. Each team played the other six in its group once in a round-robin format. The top four sides from each group qualified for the quarter-finals.

Mascot: Stumpy the elephant

Prize money: US$ 8,000,000

Prize money for the winners: US$ 3,200,000

Groups –

A: Pakistan, Sri Lanka, Australia, New Zealand, Zimbabwe, Canada, Kenya

B: South Africa, India, England, West Indies, Bangladesh, Ireland, Netherlands

Winners: India

Runners-up: Sri Lanka

Losing semi-finalists: New Zealand (lost to Sri Lanka) and Pakistan (lost to India)

Highest scorer: Tillakaratne Dilshan (Sri Lanka)—500 runs @62.5 from nine matches, inclusive of 2 hundreds and 2 fifties

Dilshan's highest score: 158 v Zimbabwe at Kandy

Highest wicket-takers:

Shahid Afridi (Pakistan)—21 wickets @12.85 from eight matches, inclusive of two 5-wicket hauls and two 4-wicket hauls

2011: DHONI'S DEVILS

Afridi's best bowling figures: 5/16 v Kenya at Hambantota
Zaheer Khan (India)—21 wickets @18.7 from nine matches
Khan's best bowling figures: 3/20 v the Netherlands at Delhi
Player of the tournament: Yuvraj Singh (India)—362 runs and 15 wickets

CLASSIC CLASHES

Group B: Ireland v England, M. Chinnaswamy Stadium, Bengaluru, 2 March 2011

England took on their neighbours in Bengaluru, three days after chasing 338 to tie their encounter against India at the same venue. Batting first, England scored freely. Andrew Strauss, the captain, and Kevin Pietersen, his predecessor, opened the innings and put on 91. Both then fell in quick succession, but the Irish bowlers were then blunted by Jonathan Trott and Ian Bell, who added 167 for the third wicket. A total in excess of 350 looked imminent, but the Irish managed to press the brakes, conceding only 33 in the last 5 overs. The result seemed a foregone conclusion when Ireland lost their fifth wicket with only 111 on the board. However, Kevin O'Brien, Ireland's No. 6, was determined to fight to the finish. What ensued left the England players and watchers stunned. O'Brien unleashed one of the most breathtaking assaults in World Cup history. He found an ally in Alex Cusack, who contributed 47 to a sixth-wicket stand of 162. O'Brien completed 100 in 50 balls, the fastest in World Cup history. By the time he was run out for 113, the equation was down to 11 runs from the same number of deliveries. John Mooney, who had essayed an excellent supporting hand after Cusack's dismissal, was at the wrong end. However, Trent Johnston, the former captain, settled Irish nerves with a boundary off the first ball he faced. Mooney and he completed the highest successful chase in World Cup history with 5 balls to spare.

Result: England [327/8 (50)] lost to Ireland [329/7 (49.1)] by 3 wickets.

Group B: South Africa v India, VCA Stadium, Jamtha, Nagpur, 12 March 2011

Mahendra Singh Dhoni won the toss and elected to bat. The capacity crowd could not stop cheering as Sachin Tendulkar and Virender Sehwag toyed with one of the best bowling attacks in the world. The openers scored at more than a run a ball and Gautam Gambhir, who replaced Sehwag, ensured that the runs kept coming. When Tendulkar completed his 48th ODI century, the South Africans were staring at a possibility of being 'batted' out of the match even before their batsmen had padded up. However, they came back with a vengeance, their

2011: DHONI'S DEVILS

cause being helped by shoddy shot-selection. India collapsed from 267/1 in the 40th over to 296 (all out) in the penultimate over. Hashim Amla and Jacques Kallis batted well together in response, but India managed to stay ahead. When Kallis was third out in the 36th over, South Africa needed 124 more in 86 balls. Their middle order then did what the Indian middle order hadn't. AB de Villiers stepped on the accelerator, and JP Duminy and Johan Botha also displayed enterprise, but it still appeared that it wouldn't be enough. When Botha fell in the 48th over, the target was still 18 runs away. Faf du Plessis and Rob Peterson took the match into the final over, with 13 still needed. Peterson inside-edged Ashish Nehra's first ball for a four and then banged the second over long-on for a six. The third ball yielded 2 runs and Peterson smashed the fourth ball through the covers to take his team home.

Result: India [296 (48.4)] lost to South Africa [300/7 (49.4)] by 3 wickets.

Second quarter-final: India v Australia, Sardar Patel Gujarat Stadium, Motera, Ahmedabad, 24 March 2011

Ricky Ponting led from the front after winning the toss, with an innings of 104. India opened the bowling with Ravichandran Ashwin, the off-spinner, and largely did well. A target of 261 was competitive but not intimidating for one of the best batting line-ups in the world. Sehwag and Tendulkar put on 44 before

Shane Watson made the breakthrough. Tendulkar added a further 50 with Gambhir before falling, soon after completing his half century. Although Virat Kohli, the new man at the crease, looked assured, the Indians lost their way a bit in the middle overs. Gambhir reached his 50 after Kohli's dismissal but found himself having communication issues with Yuvraj Singh. He was run out after a couple of near-misses. When Dhoni, a master at marshalling chases, fell to a catch at point off Brett Lee, the match was evenly poised—India needed 74 runs from 75 balls with 5 wickets in hand. Suresh Raina, who was playing his first match of the tournament, came in and gave Yuvraj Singh the support the southpaw from Punjab deserved. The hero of India's victorious campaigns in the Under-19 World Cup in 2000 and the ICC World T20 2007 was outstanding. He remained unbeaten on 57, finishing off the match with a cover drive boundary and a roar of delight. It was the first time since 1992 that Australia had not made it to at least the semi-finals of a World Cup.

Result: Australia [260/6 (50)] lost to India [261/5 (47.4)] by 5 wickets.

Final: India v Sri Lanka, Wankhede Stadium, Mumbai, 2 April 2011

The summit clash began with confusion at the toss; Ravi Shastri, the TV presenter, announced that Mahendra Singh Dhoni, who

2011: DHONI'S DEVILS

tossed the coin, had won it, but Jeff Crowe, the match referee, said that he hadn't heard the call of Kumara Sangakkara, the Sri Lankan captain. The coin was tossed again and Sangakkara won and elected to bat. Zaheer Khan, who had conceded 15 runs in the first over of the 2003 World Cup, began the 2011 final with a spell that read 5-3-6-1. The Sri Lankan batting was largely subdued until Mahela Jayawardene took charge. His 103 helped Sri Lanka total 274/6. India's Virender Sehwag fell on the second ball and the galleries fell silent when Sachin Tendulkar was caught behind with only 31 runs on the board. Gautam Gambhir then stepped up a gear to essay a masterpiece, considering what was at stake. He added 83 with Virat Kohli before the latter was brilliantly caught-and-bowled by Tillakaratne Dilshan. Dhoni promoted himself in the batting order ahead of Yuvraj Singh to take on and tackle Sri Lanka's slow bowlers, led as they were by the redoubtable Muttiah Muralitharan. The move paid off. The spectators got more and more animated as the target got nearer. Gambhir was only 3 runs short of what would have been an epic hundred when he was bowled off an inside-edge. He was replaced by Yuvraj, who complemented his captain stroke-for-stroke. 4 were needed from 11 balls when Dhoni swung Nuwan Kulasekhara over long-on to seal India's second World Cup triumph.

Result: Sri Lanka [274/6 (50)] lost to India [277/4 (48.2)] by 6 wickets.

THE 2011 WORLD CUP QUIZ

1. Who were the two centurions in the only Group B match to end in a tie?
2. Name the bowler whom Virender Sehwag struck for a boundary off the first ball of the first match of the tournament.
3. What happened on 23 May 1999 that happened next on 19 March 2011?
4. Which team was bowled out for double-digit scores twice in the tournament?
5. How many 'Player of the Match' awards did Yuvraj Singh, the Player of the Tournament, win in the competition?
6. Name the Netherlands player who scored 2 centuries in the competition.
7. Who produced the best bowling figures of the tournament?
8. My team did not qualify for the semi-finals, but I still finished as the fourth-highest scorer in the tournament. The three batsmen who outscored me belonged to teams that went all the way to the final. Who am I?
9. Who in 2011 became the second cricketer after Javed Miandad to appear in six World Cups?
10. Two of the four quarter-finals ended with a 10-wicket win. Sri Lanka beat England by that margin at Colombo. Which teams were involved in the other match?

2011: DHONI'S DEVILS

THE 2011 WORLD CUP QUIZ: ANSWERS

1. The Group B encounter between India and England was tied. Sachin Tendulkar and Andrew Strauss were the centurions in the match.
2. Shafiul Islam of Bangladesh
3. A defeat suffered by Australia in a World Cup match. Australia lost to Pakistan by 10 runs at Leeds in a Group B encounter of the 1999 World Cup on 23 May 1999. The Australians went on to win six matches and tie one in the 1999 World Cup and were unbeaten in the 2003 and 2007 World Cups (eleven matches each). They then won four group matches out of five in the 2011 World Cup (one match was abandoned). Coincidentally, their unbeaten streak ended with a 4-wicket loss to Pakistan at Colombo on 19 March 2011 in their sixth and last Group A match.
4. Bangladesh were dismissed for 58 and 78 by the West Indies and South Africa respectively. Both league matches were played at Mirpur.
5. Yuvraj Singh won four of these awards. He won the individual award in the Group B matches against Ireland, the Netherlands and the West Indies and in the quarter-final against Australia.
6. Ryan ten Doeschate scored 119 against England at Nagpur and 106 against Ireland at Kolkata.

7. Kemar Roach of the West Indies took 6/27 against the Netherlands at Delhi.
8. England's Jonathan Trott was the fourth-highest scorer of the tournament with 422 runs @60.2 from seven matches. Ahead of him on the table were two Sri Lankans—Tillakaratne Dilshan (top scorer) and Kumara Sangakkara (third-highest scorer) and one Indian—Sachin Tendulkar (second-highest scorer).
9. Sachin Tendulkar
10. Pakistan beat the West Indies by 10 wickets at Dhaka.

11

2015: ADVANCE AUSTRALIA!

THERE WAS TALK of the eleventh World Cup featuring ten teams, but the ICC eventually decided to proceed on the same lines as the 2011 edition. For the second successive time, co-hosts faced off in the summit clash. New Zealand made their first appearance in a World Cup final, only to be outplayed by their Trans-Tasman rivals, who won the title for the fifth time. Scotland and the United Arab Emirates, the top two teams in the 2014 World Cup qualifier, made it to the competition. Afghanistan and Ireland, the top two teams in the 2011-13 ICC World Cricket League, qualified directly. The tournament was played in an era in which the sport's shortest format, which was introduced in England in 2003, had captured the imagination of fans across the world. The Indian Premier League, which had been in existence since 2008, had inspired a host of leagues in other countries, Australia included. The impact of T20 cricket was evident in the 2015 edition of the World Cup; as many as twenty-eight scores in excess of 300 were posted in the competition, three of which were in excess of 400. There were five matches in which both the teams crossed 300 runs. To put these figures in perspective, the 2003, 2007 and 2011 editions of the World Cup had witnessed nine, sixteen and seventeen scores above 300 respectively. Two batsmen—Martin Guptill of New Zealand and Chris Gayle of the West Indies—scored double centuries in the tournament. It was obvious that the authorities needed to do something to bridge the rapidly widening gap between the bat and the ball.

FACTFILE: ICC CRICKET WORLD CUP 2015

Hosts: Australia and New Zealand
Duration: 14 February–29 March
Participating teams: 14
Matches: 49
Venues: 14 (7 each in Australia and New Zealand)
Trophy: Rotating trophy

2015: ADVANCE AUSTRALIA!

Format: The fourteen teams were divided into two groups of seven teams each. Each team played the other six in its group once in a round-robin format. The top four sides from each group qualified for the quarter-finals.

Prize money: US$ 10,000,000

Prize money for the winners: US$ 3,975,000 (US$ 4,020,000 if the team was unbeaten in the competition)

Groups –

A: **New Zealand, Australia, Sri Lanka, Bangladesh**, England, Afghanistan, Scotland

B: **India, South Africa, Pakistan, West Indies**, Ireland, Zimbabwe, United Arab Emirates

Winners: Australia

Runners-up: New Zealand

Losing semi-finalists: India (lost to Australia) and South Africa (lost to New Zealand)

Highest scorer: Martin Guptill (New Zealand)—547 runs @68.3 from nine matches, inclusive of 2 centuries and a fifty

Guptill's highest score: 237* v West Indies at Wellington

Highest wicket-takers:

Mitchell Starc (Australia)—22 wickets @10.1 from eight matches, inclusive of one 5-wicket haul and one 4-wicket haul

Starc's best bowling figures: 6/28 v New Zealand at Auckland

Trent Boult (New Zealand)—22 wickets @16.8 from nine matches, inclusive of one 5-wicket haul and one 4-wicket haul

Boult's best bowling figures: 5/27 v Australia at Auckland (in the same match as above)

Player of the tournament: Mitchell Starc

CLASSIC CLASHES

Group B: New Zealand v Australia, Eden Park, Auckland, 28 February 2015

Australia won the toss and batted against their co-hosts. Aaron Finch's dismissal at 30 brought in Shane Watson, and he and David Warner added a brisk 50 before both fell off consecutive deliveries. The twin strikes sparked off a slide and the four-time champions were bowled out for 151. The first half of the New Zealand innings, which began before the scheduled mid-innings break, turned out to be a near-replica of the Australian. Brendon McCullum, the Kiwi captain, began with a bang and completed his 50 before falling to Pat Cummins just before the break. Ross Taylor and Grant Elliott perished on either side of the interval, before Corey Anderson steadied the boat. He scored 26 before falling to Glenn Maxwell's off spinner. New Zealand at that stage were comfortably placed, needing only 21 more with 5 wickets in hand, but the Australians gave it everything. Luke Ronchi hit a six, but he fell with 13 needed. Daniel Vettori fell, with 7 needed, and yet another 'Great Escape' by Australia in a World Cup match seemed on the cards when Starc bowled Adam Milne and Tim Southee off consecutive deliveries. The target was still 6 runs away. Boult, the No. 11, prevented a hat trick and left it to Kane Williamson, who had kept a steady head even as everything seemed to be going south at the other end. He biffed the first ball of the next over, bowled by Cummins, straight and high for a six.

Result: Australia [151 (32.2)] lost to New Zealand [152/9 (23.1)] by 1 wicket.

Third quarter-final: Australia v Pakistan, Adelaide Oval, 20 March 2015

Pakistan won the toss and opted to bat. Several batsmen got off to good starts, but not one made it count. Josh Hazlewood was the pick of the bowlers with 4 wickets as Pakistan were dismissed for a meagre 213. When the Australians began their chase, one man took it upon himself to push them onto the back foot. That evening at the Adelaide Oval, the left-handed Wahab Riaz made a statement on behalf of the entire bowling fraternity, the members of which had been treated with scant respect in the tournament. He mixed raw pace with accuracy to deliver a performance that was nothing short of lethal. His dismissals of David Warner and Michael Clarke brought Shane Watson to the crease. Watson, who had said a few uncomplimentary things to Riaz when the latter had come in to bat earlier in the day, was marked out for special attention and posed question after uncomfortable question with the ball. Riaz's perseverance paid off when Watson mis-hooked him in his 5th over. Unfortunately for Riaz and his team, their glee at seeing Rahat Ali positioning himself under the ball was short-lived, as the fielder spilt a sitter. The drop deflated Riaz and the Pakistanis and invigorated the Australians, who proceeded to complete a 6-wicket win with 17 overs to spare. Watson deserved all the credit he got for not losing his composure despite getting a thorough working-over and capitalizing on the reprieve to remain unbeaten at 64.

Result: Pakistan [213 (49.5)] lost to Australia [216/4 (33.5)] by 6 wickets.

First semi-final: New Zealand v South Africa, Eden Park, Auckland, 24 March 2015

Batting first, South Africa were sitting pretty at 216/3 from 38 overs, with Faf du Plessis and AB de Villiers going great guns when a shower resulted in the match being truncated to 43-overs-a-side. David Miller's belligerence helped the Proteas finish at 281/5. New Zealand's target was revised to 298, as per the D/L calculations. McCullum provided his team with

2015: ADVANCE AUSTRALIA!

yet another blazing start, but Morne Morkel played spoilsport by dismissing the Kiwi captain after the latter had contributed 59 to an opening stand of 71. Martin Guptill and Ross Taylor fell in their thirties, but Grant Elliott and Corey Anderson, who came together at 149/4, made their outings count. Anderson made the most of a missed run out chance when he was on 33 and took the lead in a partnership of 103, which ended with his falling to Morkel. Elliott was in the zone and batting magnificently, but it did appear that he would run out of deliveries. Daniel Vettori replaced Luke Ronchi in the middle with 29 needed off 17 balls, and the last over began with the co-hosts still needing 12. A bye and a single brought Vettori on strike to face Dale Steyn's third ball. The former Kiwi captain stroked a boundary on the off side and scampered for a bye off the next delivery. Elliott, back on strike with 5 needed from 2 balls, sighted Steyn's fifth ball early, retreated into the crease and swung hard. The ball cleared long-on.

Result: South Africa [281/5 (43)] lost to New Zealand [299/6 (42.5)] by 4 wickets (D/L method).

Final: Australia v New Zealand, Melbourne Cricket Ground, 29 March 2015

The first-time finalists appeared overawed, played as if they were overwhelmed, and were consequently outplayed. Brendon McCullum, their captain and talisman, was bowled by Starc for a duck in the very first over, after he had won the toss and elected to bat. Martin Guptill was second out at 33, bowled by Glenn Maxwell. Kane Williamson, the hero of the previous Trans-Tasman face-off in the tournament, was caught-and-bowled by Mitchell Johnson. The Australians were relentless with the ball and in the field. Ross Taylor and Grant Elliott added 111 for the fourth wicket, but they never seemed in control. The innings hurtled towards a premature end once Taylor fell to James Faulkner. A score of 183 in a World Cup final rekindled memories of 1983, but that turned out to be the first of only two similarities between the eleventh World Cup final and the third. The early dismissal of the chasing side's opener was the second. Aaron Finch fell with only 2 runs on the board, but David Warner was his usual belligerent self until he was dismissed at 63. Steve Smith was then joined at the wicket by his captain Michael Clarke, who had announced that he would be retiring from ODIs at the end of the tournament. Clarke and the man who would be his successor applied the finishing touches to the efforts of their bowlers, with a stand of 112. Clarke became the fourth Australian captain after Allan Border, Steve Waugh and Ricky Ponting to lead his team to World Cup glory.

Result: New Zealand [183 (45)] lost to Australia [186/3 (33.1)] by 7 wickets.

2015: ADVANCE AUSTRALIA!

THE 2015 WORLD CUP QUIZ

1. Which was the only match of the competition to be abandoned without a ball being bowled?
2. Who was India's highest scorer of the tournament?
3. Which team set a record for the highest total in a World Cup match, in the competition?
4. Name the player who scored a record 4 consecutive centuries in the tournament.
5. Which team posted two totals that were 400-plus in the tournament?
6. Name the pair that added a record 372 for the second wicket against Zimbabwe in a group match.
7. What did the first five matches of the tournament have in common?
8. I was the Player of the Under-19 World Cup in 2008 and the second-highest wicket-taker in the 2011 World Cup. I took 7/33 in a group match of the 2015 World Cup. Who am I?
9. Who was the second-highest wicket-taker of the tournament after the joint toppers Starc and Boult?
10. I scored a century and 3 fifties and hit 21 sixes in the competition. Who am I?

THE TRAIL OF CRICKET'S HOLY GRAIL

THE 2015 WORLD CUP QUIZ: ANSWERS

1. The Group A match between Australia and Bangladesh at Brisbane
2. Shikhar Dhawan, who scored 412 runs @ 51.5 from eight matches.
3. Australia's 417/6 against Afghanistan at Perth was the highest total in a World Cup match, ahead of India's 413/5 against Bermuda in the 2007 World Cup.
4. Kumara Sangakkara (Sri Lanka) scored 105* against Bangladesh, 117* against England, 104 against Australia and 124 against Scotland.
5. South Africa scored 408/5 against the West Indies at Sydney and 411/4 against Ireland at Canberra.
6. Chris Gayle and Marlon Samuels of the West Indies. Their stand of 372 is the highest-ever partnership in ODIs.
7. The team batting first scored 300-plus in each of the first five matches.
8. Tim Southee (New Zealand) took 7/33 against England at Wellington.
9. Umesh Yadav (India) was the second-highest wicket-taker with a tally of 18 from eight matches.
10. AB de Villiers (South Africa)

12

INDIA V PAKISTAN: SIX OUT OF SIX!

The ODI rivalry between India and Pakistan can be divided into three distinct phases. Phase I spans the period from their first ODI, played at Quetta in October 1978, which India won by 4 runs, to the final of the Austral-Asia Cup at Sharjah in April 1986, which Pakistan won by 1 wicket, thanks to an extraordinary innings by Javed Miandad. Honours were even during this phase, with both sides winning eight matches each. The massive psychological boost that Miandad's heroics in that Austral-Asia Cup final—especially his last-ball six to win the match for his team—gave Pakistan, was evident in Phase II, which lasted for more than a decade and a half. Pakistan won forty-four matches to India's twenty-two in this period. It took another epic innings—this time by Sachin Tendulkar in the 2003 World Cup encounter at Centurion on 1 March 2003—to break Pakistan's mental stranglehold. Phase III, which spans the period from 2004 to 2018, saw the Indians edging ahead in the head-to-head equation, with twenty-four wins to Pakistan's twenty-one. Cumulatively, Pakistan are way ahead with seventy-three wins to India's fifty-four, but the quadrennial event has a different story to tell. All six World Cup matches between the two have been won by India, notwithstanding the fact that four of those were played during the Pakistan-dominated Phase II. Not surprisingly, the individual award in three of the six matches was won by Sachin Tendulkar, India's cricketing colossus for a quarter of a century.

Match 1: League—Sydney Cricket Ground, 4 March 1992

The neighbours played each other for the first time in a World Cup in the fifth edition of the competition. The Indians, who won the toss and elected to bat, were not allowed to score freely. Ajay Jadeja scored 46 and Azharuddin got 32, but it was the nineteen-year-old Sachin Tendulkar who broke the shackles. His partnership with the veteran Kapil Dev in the end overs enabled India to finish at a competitive 216/7. Pakistan lost 2 early wickets in response, but the innings was stabilized by Aamir Sohail and Javed Miandad. Even as the battle of attrition

INDIA V PAKISTAN: SIX OUT OF SIX!

raged on, Miandad found himself exchanging words with Kiran More, India's wicketkeeper, the grand culmination of which was the Pakistani legend's impersonation of More by imitating his style of appealing. Tendulkar produced the breakthrough for India when he had Sohail caught at short mid-wicket, shortly after Pakistan had crossed 100. Salim Malik hit a couple of boundaries, but once he was caught behind off Manoj Prabhakar, the Indians took control. The Pakistani middle order fell apart against some excellent bowling and fielding. Imran Khan was run out, Wasim Akram stumped and Miandad bowled by Javagal Srinath. Moin Khan, the Pakistani keeper-batsman, sparkled in a cameo before he was caught in the deep. The final wicket fell in the final over. Pakistan had collapsed from 105/2 to 173 (all out). That they picked themselves up and went on to win the tournament is a different story.

Result: India [216/7 (49)] beat Pakistan [173 (48.1)] by 43 runs.

Match 2: Second quarter-final—M. Chinnaswamy Stadium, Bengaluru, 9 March 1996

The capacity crowd exploded when it was announced that India had won the toss and elected to bat. The batsmen did well, but the Pakistani bowlers kept a tab on the scoring. Tendulkar contributed 31 to an opening stand of 90. Navjot Sidhu, his partner, scored 93, and Azharuddin and Vinod Kambli fell just when they were looking ominous. India were at 226/5 at the end of the 46th over and it seemed that they would just about manage to cross 250. Ajay Jadeja then rewrote the script with a breathtaking assault. Waqar Younis, Pakistan's spearhead in the absence of their indisposed captain, Wasim Akram, was hit for 40 runs in his last 2 overs. The carnage continued after the mid-innings break, courtesy Saeed Anwar and Aamir Sohail, the Pakistani openers. The scoring rate was well above 8 an over when Anwar fell, but Sohail carried on in the same vein until he decided to attack Venkatesh Prasad, India's new-ball bowler, with his mouth instead of his bat. Prasad had the last laugh. His dismissal of Sohail to an overambitious shot was just the opening India had been looking for. Pounded into submission in the initial overs, the bowlers came back with a vengeance. Wickets were taken at regular intervals and the match kept getting further and further away from Pakistan. Javed Miandad, India's nemesis in many an encounter between the two teams, was run out in what was the last match of his career.

Result: India 287/8 (50) beat Pakistan 248/9 (49)[4] by 39 runs.

---

[4]Pakistan were docked one over for not completing the full quota of overs in the stipulated time

INDIA V PAKISTAN: SIX OUT OF SIX!

Match 3: Fourth Super Six match—Old Trafford, Manchester, 8 June 1999

This match was played when the armies of the two nations were battling each other on the peaks of Kargil. Pakistan were better placed than India in the tournament rankings and could afford a loss, while India's prospects of making it to the semis looked bleak. Not only did they need to win the match, but they also needed other results to go their way. India's luck with the toss against Pakistan in World Cup matches continued in the 1999 edition. They batted first and totalled 227/6, thanks to half centuries by Mohammed Azharuddin and Rahul Dravid, and a knock of 45 by Tendulkar. Javagal Srinath then gave his team a great start with the ball, dismissing Shahid Afridi and Ijaz Ahmed, the latter to a brilliant catch by Azharuddin. Prasad and Kumble also chipped in, and at 78/5, Pakistan were in more than a spot of bother. Moin Khan, who had had a memorable tournament with the bat, gave his team hope with a run-a-ball knock, which ended when he clipped Prasad uppishly and was caught in the deep by Tendulkar. Pakistan did not recover from the setback, Prasad's dismissal of Inzamam-ul-Haq for 41 being the last straw. They were all out for 180, and Prasad, who had finished with figures of 5/27, his best in ODIs, was carried off the field by ecstatic Indian fans. As had happened in 1992, Pakistan went all the way to the final, despite the defeat.

Result: India [227/6 (50)] beat Pakistan [180 (45.3)] by 47 runs.

Match 4: Pool A—Supersport Park, Centurion, 1 March 2003

The lead-up to the match saw a reversal of roles from 1999; while India were assured of a place in the Super Six, Pakistan were on the brink of elimination. Saeed Anwar, who had destroyed the Indian bowling on several occasions in the 1990s, contributed 101 to Pakistan's 273/7. Considering that India's highest successful chase in a World Cup match at that point was 222, history seemed to be on Pakistan's side at the mid-innings interval. After Wasim Akram's first over yielded two boundaries, Shoaib Akhtar, the world's fastest bowler, was assigned the second. Sachin Tendulkar cut his fourth ball over point for a six. He flicked the fifth ball for a boundary and then timed a defensive push off the sixth so well that the ball sped to the fence. India were up and galloping. The dismissals of Virender Sehwag and Sourav Ganguly off consecutive deliveries did not faze Tendulkar, who was at his emphatic best. Mohammed Kaif, who came in at No. 4, helped his senior partner keep the scoreboard buzzing till he played on to Shahid Afridi in the 22nd over. The score was 153/3 at that stage and India were well ahead of the required rate. Tendulkar started cramping as he neared a century, and a runner was eventually requisitioned.

INDIA V PAKISTAN: SIX OUT OF SIX!

The master was caught off Shoaib for 98, with 97 still needed. Rahul Dravid and Yuvraj Singh, both of whom were at their unflustered best, took India home with more than 4 overs to spare.

Result: Pakistan [273/7 (50)] lost to India [276/4 (45.4)] by 6 wickets.

Match 5: Second semi-final—PCA Stadium, Mohali, 30 March 2011

The full house at the venue comprised the Prime Ministers of both countries and five hundred fans from Pakistan who had crossed over into India through the Wagah border. India won the toss and elected to bat. Sachin Tendulkar got as many as four 'lives' and a reprieve courtesy the DRS in his innings of 85. India, 116/1 at one stage, were jolted by Wahab Riaz, who dismissed Virat Kohli and Yuvraj Singh off successive balls. Indian fans feared the worst when Mahendra Singh Dhoni was the sixth man out at 205, with 9 overs left. Suresh Raina batted sensibly along with the lower order to ensure that the full 50 overs were accounted for. Riaz was Pakistan's best bowler, with figures of 5/46. Needing 261 to win, Pakistan made a good beginning and crossed 100 for the loss of only 2 wickets, but Yuvraj Singh then made a double strike, dismissing Asad Shafiq and the experienced Younis Khan in quick succession. Umar Akmal looked impressive until he was bowled by Harbhajan

Singh. This was the point at which the match swung decisively in India's favour. Misbah-ul-Haq stroked his way to a half century, but he did not get the support he deserved from the Pakistani lower order. India had reason to be pleased with their performance with the ball and in the field. All five bowlers used by Dhoni—Zaheer Khan, Ashish Nehra, Munaf Patel, Harbhajan Singh and Yuvraj Singh—took 2 wickets each.

Result: India [260/9 (50)] beat Pakistan [231 (49.5)] by 29 runs.

Match 6: Group B—Adelaide Oval, 15 February 2015

India commenced their defence of their 2011 title with a bout against their traditional rivals. Mahendra Singh Dhoni won the toss and gave his batsmen first use of the Adelaide wicket. After Rohit Sharma fell early, Virat Kohli batted brilliantly in the company of Shikhar Dhawan, the other opener. The duo added 129 for the second wicket and Suresh Raina, who replaced Dhawan at the crease, maintained the momentum in association with Kohli. India's vice-captain eventually fell after scoring 107. Pakistan bowled well at the end and India finished with 300/7, at least 25 runs short of what they would have aimed for after the two century-plus partnerships. As had been the case in the previous World Cup clash between the two teams, a Pakistani paceman—Sohail Khan in this match—took 5 wickets. The similarities with the 2011 semi-final at Mohali did not end there. Pakistan once

INDIA V PAKISTAN: SIX OUT OF SIX!

again got off to a steady start but lost their way just after 100 had been posted. Three specialist batsmen fell for the addition of only 1 run. Ahmed Shehzad and Sohail Maqsood were dismissed by Umesh Yadav and Ravindra Jadeja had Umar Akmal caught behind. The Indians proceeded to deny the subsequent batsmen the room to play in. Misbah-ul-Haq, Pakistan's batting hero in the 2011 semi-final, scored 76, but his was yet again a lone battle. Pakistan lost their final wicket with 3 overs left.

Result: India [300/7 (50)] beat Pakistan [224 (47)] by 76 runs.

THE 'INDIA V PAKISTAN' WORLD CUP QUIZ

1. In how many countries have India and Pakistan played against each other in the World Cup?
2. Name the umpires who stood in the first India-Pakistan match in the World Cup.
3. Who led India in three of the six World Cup matches against Pakistan?
4. Four of the six World Cup matches between India and Pakistan were day/night encounters. The 1999 match at Manchester was one of two 'day' World Cup matches between the two teams. Which was the other 'day' match?
5. Rashid Latif, Pakistan's wicketkeeper in the ICC CWC 2003, sustained a head injury while batting in the match against India, and could not keep wicket during India's

innings as a result. Who stood behind the stumps for Pakistan in his place?
6. Fill in the blanks: Imran Khan, _____, Wasim Akram, Waqar Younis, _____, Misbah-ul-Haq.
7. Name the only player from among the following who appeared in only one of the six India-Pakistan matches in the World Cup—Javed Miandad, Sourav Ganguly, Sanjay Manjrekar, Virat Kohli, Moin Khan.
8. Which Indian bowler took a total of 8 wickets in two World Cup matches against Pakistan?
9. Who was India's best bowler in the 2015 encounter?
10. Who briefly appeared as Sachin Tendulkar's runner in the 2003 World Cup match?

THE 'INDIA V PAKISTAN' WORLD CUP QUIZ: ANSWERS

1. Four countries. They played each other twice in India and Australia, and once each in England and South Africa.
2. David Shepherd (England) and Peter McConnell (Australia)
3. Mohammed Azharuddin led India in the 1992, 1996 and 1999 matches.
4. The 2003 match at Centurion, South Africa
5. Taufeeq Umar

INDIA V PAKISTAN: SIX OUT OF SIX!

6. Pakistan's captains in World Cup matches against India in chronological order. The missing ones are Aamir Sohail (1996) and Shahid Afridi (2011).
7. Sourav Ganguly played in only the 2003 match.
8. Venkatesh Prasad took 3/45 in 1996 and 5/27 in 1999.
9. Mohammed Shami, who took 4/35
10. Virender Sehwag

13

2019—BACK TO BLIGHTY

We want the World Cup to not just be window-dressing but a shop window for cricket at the highest level... Now we realize, let's not spread ourselves out too thin, we've got full member countries, Zimbabwe being one, West Indies maybe, where we've got to be careful that they don't fall off the ship.

—David Richardson, Chief Executive,
International Cricket Council
(quoted on www.cricket.com.au, 26 March 2015)

THE TWELFTH WORLD Cup and fifth to be hosted by England will be the first to feature ten teams. The ICC was criticised for reducing the number of participants, especially by Associate Member nations, who alluded to the possibility of none of them qualifying for the tournament. However, the apex body has reiterated that it knows what it is doing. While the ICC remains committed to its objective to popularize the game across the globe, it has taken a conscious decision to prioritize the tackling of challenges that are being encountered in regions where the game already has a presence. The decision to limit the number of teams in the premier quadrennial competition is part of an endeavour to promote quality at the expense of quantity.

As per the revised World Cup qualification guidelines, England (hosts) and seven other top teams in the ICC's ODI ranking on 30 September 2017 automatically qualified for the 2019 edition. The full members of the ICC who missed out on a direct entry were the West Indies and Zimbabwe, as also Afghanistan and Ireland, both of whom were given 'Test' status in 2017 and played their inaugural Tests in 2018. These four teams had to participate in the 2018 Cricket World Cup Qualifier along with many others. The ICC has not spared any effort over the years to make the World Cup Qualifier a robust tournament, which in turn has enhanced the possibility of associate members getting the better of full members who may not qualify directly. As it transpired, Afghanistan and the West Indies reached the final of the Qualifier and made the grade, but Zimbabwe and Ireland missed out. Their absence will make the ICC CWC 2019 the first World Cup not to feature all the member-nations.

FACTFILE: ICC CRICKET WORLD CUP 2019

Hosts: England and Wales

Duration: 30 May–14 July

Participating teams: 10

Matches: 48

Venues: 11 (10 in England and 1 in Wales)

Trophy: Rotating trophy

Format: Each team will play the other nine once in a round-robin league. The top four sides at the end of the league will qualify for the semi-finals.

Prize money: US$ 14,000,000

Prize money for the winners: US$ 4,800,000

THE A–Z OF THE ICC CWC 2019

A – Australia: The defending champions lost eleven ODIs and won just two in the calendar year of 2018. 2019 did not start on a happy note for them either, with a 1-2 loss to India in an ODI series. Nevertheless, only a fool will underestimate the

2019—BACK TO BLIGHTY

five-time winners when the twelfth World Cup gets underway. Steve Smith and David Warner, both of whom were part of Michael Clarke's squad that won the title in 2015, will be part of the squad after serving their one-year bans. The duo will want to make up for lost time.

B – Birmingham: The city and its venue (Edgbaston) will be remembered for two stirring World Cup matches—the one-wicket heist that Deryck Murray and Andy Roberts pulled off for the West Indies against Pakistan in 1975, and the incredible 1999 World Cup semi-final between Australia and South Africa. Edgbaston will be hosting five matches of the 2019 World Cup, including the second semi-final.

C – Cardiff: The Sophia Gardens in the capital of Wales made its ODI debut in the 1999 World Cup. The venue hosted a solitary match between Australia and New Zealand, which the Kiwis won by 5 wickets. The venue will be hosting four league matches of the 2019 edition.

D – Dhoni: It is being speculated that the man who led India to World Cup glory in 2011 will hang up his boots for good after the 2019 edition. But then, MSD, who has always lived in the 'here and the now', has never allowed emotion to overshadow pragmatism. The Player of the ODI series that India won in

Australia in January 2019 will do everything he can, in front of the stumps, behind them and cerebrally, to ensure that Team India repeats its performance of 2011, in the twelfth World Cup. Thoughts of retirement, if any, will not be entertained when the competition is in progress.

E – England: They reached the final thrice in the first five editions of the World Cup but didn't make it to even the semi-finals since. It is ironic that the country where cricket was born has only one international title—the ICC World T20 2010—to show. Fans of the team will hope that the players create history on home turf.

F – Fakhar Zaman: India enjoyed a cent per cent success record in the 2017 edition of the ICC Champions Trophy, which was played in England. That made them the favourites in the summit clash against Pakistan, but one man changed the complexion of the match with a brilliant and ultimately match-winning 114. Pakistan will pray that their star opener replicates that performance in the ICC CWC 2019.

G – Groups: The 2019 edition will be the first World Cup since 1992 without 'groups' or 'pools'. Each team will play as many as nine league matches—one against every other team in the fray. The format will give teams that do not start well a chance of returning into contention. On the other hand, there will be a possibility of a team or two peaking too early, like England in 1992.

H – Hampshire: The magnificent Rose Bowl at Southampton in the county of Hampshire will make its World Cup debut in the upcoming edition. The venue will host five matches in all, including India's first match of the tournament, against South Africa at Southampton on 5 June.

I – Imran Tahir: A member of the Pakistani team that played in the ICC Under-19 CWC in 1998, the leg spinner subsequently shifted to South Africa and made his ODI debut against the West Indies at Delhi in the ICC CWC 2011. He has done well since. One of the most respected contemporary cricketers, Imran presently shares the South African record for the fastest 150 wickets in ODIs (eighty-nine matches) with Allan Donald.

J – Jasons: Jason Holder, the all-rounder from Barbados, led the West Indies in the ICC CWC 2015. He led from the front with bat and ball in the 2018 World Cup Qualifier and ensured that his team made it to the twelfth World Cup. He will be one of the players to watch out for in the tournament, along with England's Jason Roy, whose record as opener since his ODI debut in 2015 has been impressive.

K – Kayes (Imrul): The left-handed opener is expected to be a key cog in Bangladesh's wheel in the ICC CWC 2019. He made a successful return to international cricket in the 2018 Asia Cup after a couple of forgettable seasons, and aggregated 349 runs in a three-match ODI series against Zimbabwe in October 2018.

L – Lord's: The 'Mecca of Cricket' has hosted more World Cup finals (four) than any other venue. The venue that witnessed the thriller that was the 1975 final and India's incredible win in the summit clash of 1983 will host the final of the upcoming edition as well, on 14 July 2019. The final apart, Lord's will host four league matches, including the clash between Australia and England, the game's oldest rivals.

M – Mitchell Starc: The Player of the ICC CWC 2015 will not figure in the 2019 season of the IPL, which will precede the World Cup. The hiatus will ensure that the paceman who took 22 wickets in the eleventh World Cup will be fresh and raring to go in the twelfth. Mitchell Starc will lead Australia's defence of its 2015 title with the ball.

N – New Zealand: One of the most consistent outfits in World Cup history, the Kiwis have reached at least the semi-finals of a World Cup seven times out of eleven. They broke a jinx of sorts in the 2015 edition by advancing to the final for the first time. Their supporters will pray that their side improves upon its 2015 performance by going the distance in 2019.

O – Oval: The oldest Test venue on English soil and the second home of the game in the city of London will host five league matches of the ICC CWC 2019, including the inaugural match of the tournament between England and South Africa on 30 May 2019.

P – Pakistan: Sarfraz Ahmed's team created a sensation with its victory in the ICC Champions Trophy 2017, which was also played in England. They will remind themselves of that competition, especially their victory over arch-rivals India in the final, as well as the dream run of Wasim Akram's team that reached the final of the previous World Cup to be played in England.

Q – Queen: Queen Elizabeth II, the British monarch and Head of the Commonwealth of Nations, has graced many a cricket match in England and overseas with her presence over the decades. She has met and interacted with several generations of cricketers. The cricketers knighted by her include Garry Sobers, Ian Botham and Richard Hadlee, three of the greatest all-rounders of all time. The twelfth World Cup will be the fifth to be played in England during her reign, which commenced in 1953.

R – Rashid Khan: An accomplished practitioner of leg spin, cricket's most fascinating art, Rashid Khan has excelled in his brief international and league career. His performances in the 2018 World Cup qualifier played a big part in Afghanistan qualifying for the ICC CWC 2019. With a cricketer like him in the squad, no one should be surprised if the Afghans pull off a surprise or two in the tournament.

S – Steyn: One of the greatest fast bowlers of all time will be playing in his third World Cup. Dale Steyn was one of the chief architects of South Africa's 2-1 triumph in an ODI series in Australia in November 2018, with 7 wickets from three matches. South Africa will look to their spearhead to help them shed their reputation as 'chokers' for good in the ICC CWC 2019.

T – Trent Bridge and Taunton: Trent Bridge, Nottingham, will host five matches of the ICC CWC 2019, including Pakistan's first two matches of the tournament. The county ground at Taunton in Somerset will host three league matches.

U – Umbrellas: Rain, they say, is an integral part of England's cricketing culture. One can safely expect to see umbrellas at the venues, although hopefully they will stay unopened. Cricket lovers and the cricketers themselves would want showers, if any, to be brief, so that matches will not have to be curtailed or abandoned.

V – Virat: Virat Kohli led India to victory in the Under-19 ICC CWC 2008. That achievement fast-tracked his debut for the senior team. He was part of Mahendra Singh Dhoni's team that won the ICC CWC 2011 on home turf. By the time the next World Cup was played, Virat was the vice-captain of India's ODI team and one of the best batsmen on the planet. He will be one of the stars of India's campaign in 2019, if his performances on India's previous tour of England, and indeed, his penchant for excelling on the biggest stages, are anything to go by.

W – West Indies: The winners of the first two World Cups had to play the World Cup Qualifier in 2018 to get through to the ICC CWC 2019. However, things have changed since. The West Indies are a resurgent outfit. They outplayed England in a Test series in January-February 2019. The winners of the 2012 and 2016 editions of the ICC World T20 have nothing to lose and absolutely everything to gain in the twelfth World Cup.

X – Xenophobia: The ICC CWC 2019 will not be immune to the ugly side of sport. It will be represented in the form of some individuals who will go out of their way to disgrace themselves with deplorable behaviour in the venues and outside. Hopefully, this obnoxious minority will not only be outnumbered, but also out-shouted by the majority that worships cricket and treats the tournament as a celebration of the sport and the values it represents.

Y – Yorkshire: Headingley at Leeds in the county of Yorkshire witnessed two of the most outstanding bowling performances in World Cup history—Garry Gilmour's 6/14 for Australia against England in a semi-final of the 1975 edition and Winston Davis' 7/51 for the West Indies against Australia in 1983. The venue's last World Cup match was a cracker of a Super Six encounter between Australia and South Africa in 1999. The venue will host four matches in the 2019 edition, two of which will feature Afghanistan.

Z – Zimbabwe: The ICC CWC 2019 will be the first World Cup since 1979 that will not feature Zimbabwe. The side created a sensation on its World Cup debut in 1983 with a victory over Australia. The Zimbabweans entered the Super Six in 1999 and 2003 before losing their way in subsequent editions of the World Cup. They hosted the 2018 World Cup Qualifier but failed to make it to the 2019 edition after finishing third, behind Afghanistan and the West Indies.

BIBLIOGRAPHY

BOOKS

Prabhudesai, Devendra. *Around the World in Seventy-and-a-half Days*. New Delhi: Rupa, 2007.

Memon, Ayaz. *Wills Book of Excellence: One Day Cricket*. New Delhi: Orient Longman, 1992.

Ezekiel, Gulu. *The Story of World Cup Cricket*. New Delhi: Konark Publishers, 1996.

Griffiths, Edward. *Glory Days: Forty Years of One Day Cricket*. 1963–2003. New York: Viking (Penguin), 2003.

Prabhudesai, Devendra. *Hero: A Biography of Sachin Ramesh Tendulkar*. New Delhi: Rupa, 2017.

Salve, NKP. *The Story of the Reliance Cup*. New Delhi: Vikas Publishing House, 1987.

Waugh, Steve. *Out of My Comfort Zone: The Autobiography*. New

York: Viking (Penguin), 2005.
Prabhudesai, Devendra. *Cricket World Cup: Cherish and Relish.* New Delhi: Rupa, 2011.
Singh, Indra Vikram. *The Big Book of World Cup Cricket.* Sporting Links, 2011.

COMPILATIONS

Padmakar Talim Shield Tournament Golden Jubilee Commemoration Volume, Marine Sports, 1998.

NEWSPAPERS

The Times of India
The Hindu
The Indian Express
Hindustan Times
Mid-Day
DNA

MAGAZINES / PERIODICALS

Sportstar

BIBLIOGRAPHY

WEBSITES

Reuters.com
Espncricinfo.com
Rediff.com
Wikipedia.org
Tsmplug.com
News18.com
Mykhel.com
Tribune.com.pk
Totalsportek.com
Cricket.com.au
Crickex.in